THE
PROFESSION
OF ARMS

Commnent la ville de duras
fut assiettee et prinse par
sault par les francois et le
chasteau apres rendu par
composition.

leurs arbalestriers pinesa
deuant. Ainsi approucheret
ordonneement la ville. Et
bous dy bien quil y auoit
la aulains burletz dessoub
les seignrs qui sestoient p

Unt exploiterent
le duc damiou et
son ost quilz bin
drent deuant duras
Et quant ilz eurent appou

ueux deschieles p" meul
auoir lauantaige a mote
sur les murs. Si furent
plufieurs lieux es

THE PROFESSION OF ARMS

General Sir John HACKETT

MACMILLAN PUBLISHING COMPANY

NEW YORK

Macmillan Publishing Company
866 Third Avenue, New York, N.Y. 10022

Library of Congress Catalog #83-14935

First published in 1983
by Sidgwick and Jackson Limited
in Great Britain

Designed by Robert Updegraff

Picture research by Anne Horton

Page 2: Siege and capture by the French,
under the Duke of Anjou, of the town of
Duras in the Hundred Years War
(Froissart: *Chronicles*. Bibl. Nat. Fr. 2644)

10 9 8 7 6 5 4 3 2 1

Printed in the United States of America

Contents

Introduction

There must never be a general world war, a war, that is, in which the hideously effective means of mass killing and mass destruction now available are fully applied. In the whole history of mankind warfare between groups of men has never been completely unrestrained, with everything done that possibly could be done to injure or destroy an enemy. There have always been restraints upon what people will do to other people operating in some form or another, to some degree, whether formalized in agreements or emerging naturally. Such as there are at present can only be seen as totally insufficient to prevent an unimaginable calamity to mankind if the weapons we now have were exploited to even a small part of their full potential.

Man being what he is, however, conflict will continue. It is hard to conceive a future with no fighting. What has been happening ever since the Second World War, and is happening today, is not encouraging. There will be violence and those whose business is its management now assume a more important place in our societies than ever before. No one wants a nuclear holocaust. The danger is not nuclear war by grand design but nuclear war by inadvertence, into which the world has been allowed to slide through mismanagement of conflict.

The skills and qualities of the professionals in the ordered application of force now assume a greater importance in the world than ever before. In the past the survival of a nation state often depended on them. The survival of mankind may depend upon them in the future.

It is therefore of high importance to form a clear idea of what society looks for in its professional man-at-arms. To recognize what we need demands an understanding of what we have. To understand what we have we must ask how the man-at-arms came to be what he is and this in turn requires a journey into the past, into the very roots of Western culture. To see where we are going we must know where we are and to know where we are we must discover how we got here. This is an enquiry which is likely to teach lessons of close relevance to today – and tomorrow. It is the enquiry upon which we now embark.

J. W. HACKETT
Coberley Mill, Gloucestershire
September 1982

A miniature from a French ms. of c. 1390 entitled L'Arbredes Batailles *illustrating mediaeval warfare in feudal France*

Origins
of a Profession

From the beginning of man's recorded history physical force, or the threat of it, has always been freely applied to the resolution of social problems. This phenomenon seems to persist as a fundamental element in the social pattern. History suggests that as a society of men grows more orderly the application of force tends to become better ordered. The requirement for it has shown no sign of disappearing. A society regulated by force and nothing else, a completely biataxic[1] society, is probably no more than a social abstraction. It may even be a contradiction in terms. On the other hand a society of men in which there is never any resort to force at all, either for the common good or against it, either for individual advantage or against it, is inconceivable, so long as man remains what he is.

The function of the profession of arms is the ordered application of force in the resolution of a social problem. Harold Lasswell has described this function as the management of violence.[2] This is rather less precise. The bearing of arms among men for the purpose of fighting other men is found as far back as we can see. Service under arms has been seen at some times and in some places as a calling resembling that of the priesthood in its dedication. This view has never wholly disappeared. Service under arms has also been very widely regarded as a profession and also here and there, less happily, as no more than an occupation. Such service, however, has never ceased to display a strong element of the vocational.

It has evolved into a profession, not only in the wider sense of what is professed, but in the narrower sense of an occupation with a distinguishable corpus of specific technical knowledge and doctrine, a more or less exclusive group coherence, a complex of institutions peculiar to itself, an educational pattern adapted to its own specific needs, a career structure of its own and a distinct place in the society which has brought it forth. In all these respects it has strong points of resemblance to medicine and the law, as well as to holy orders. Though service under arms has strongly marked vocational elements and some (not always wholly welcome) appearances of an occupation, it is probably as a profession that it can most profitably be studied.

Roman soldiers of the Praetorian Guard, whose primary initial concern was the Emperor's personal safety. Other security functions were added. From A.D. 21–62 Praetorian troops were largely dominant over the imperial succession (Louvre)

What forms has service under arms assumed in Western societies in the past and what has been their relation to the parent society? Who joined armed forces and why? Where does the man-at-arms stand today? What can we conjecture about his place in society in the future? To questions such as these I shall attempt to suggest answers in what follows. I shall first glance at some examples of earlier forms of military institutions in Western Europe and say something of feudal soldiering. I shall then look at the regularization of military service within the framework of national standing armies. In two further chapters I shall speak of military developments in the late eighteenth century, the Napoleonic wars and the professionalization of the profession of arms which followed. I shall then say something of the American experience, not all of which in recent times has been entirely happy. I shall conclude with a general look at the military profession in the twentieth century.

I want to say something to begin with about Sparta, which offers an interesting example of a society dominated by the threat of war and given over in effect to warlike practice. In the precarious economic situation which poor soil and growing population thrust upon the communities of post-Minoan Greece Sparta made very little attempt to solve her problem by colonization or maritime adventure, or both, as others did. She chose to rely, instead, on the conquest on land of immediate neighbours. This led her, after the second and decisive Messenian war in the seventh century B.C., into the position of a garrison state.

The Spartans came to the conclusion that their survival was dependent on the subordination of almost all other considerations to military efficiency, a conclusion which was reflected in what are called the reforms of Lycurgus. Whoever or whatever Lycurgus was, what was preserved of earlier Spartan institutions was now radically adapted to meet the necessary conditions of Sparta's survival as an essentially military state.

The details of the reforms are obscure. Plutarch,[3] our chief witness, is unreliable. It is clear that the centre of the post-Lycurgan system was a *corps d'élite* of heavily armed infantrymen drawn from the whole body of the Spartiates. Each of these supported his family at a frugal level from an allotment probably cultivated by, on the average, seven Messenian serf families, *adscripti glebae*. At the battle of Plataea each Spartan hoplite in the Lacedaemonian contingent was attended by seven light-armed helots. Hoplites in other Greek contingents were each attended by one.[4] Spartiate birth, for boy or girl alike, was for those who survived infancy little more than a sentence to the ordeal of a Spartan education. Even their breeding was regulated for the purpose of producing more and better fighting men. The Spartans, according to Plutarch,[5] thought it odd that other people should put mares and bitches to the best sires they could hire or borrow but rely upon the sacred rights of husbands, even when these were feeble-minded, senile or diseased, to produce the community's crop of human offspring.

If a select body of elders decided the child was worth rearing, and should not be got rid of by exposure, it was left with its mother until the seventh year. Thereafter a Spartan boy's education was conducted for thirteen years

Spartan warrior: a bronze figure, ·15m. high, from the late sixth century B.C. The heavy cloak (the himation) under the helmet bearing its transverse crest lends grim purpose to this brooding figure, the essence of pure militarism

Spartans defeat Persian invaders at Plataea in 480 B.C., in the final collapse of the first major threat to Europe from the East

in such a way as to fit him best for the compulsory military service which would occupy him from his twenty-first year to his sixtieth. His training, though he learnt to read and write, was almost entirely moral and physical. Even the athletic sports which took so prominent a place in Hellas were largely forbidden the young Spartiate, as distracting him from more professional exercises. Sparta produced the best heavy infantry in the Hellenic world, perhaps even more feared by her neighbours than the heavy infantry of the Swiss nearly 2,000 years later. Her victories over the armies of other Greek city states were the victories of whole-time regular forces over citizen militias, the victories of a state organized primarily for war over others which were not.

Sparta achieved outstanding military distinction. The penalty, however, as is always likely to be the case where uniquely military solutions are sought to political and social problems, was a heavy one. The arts, once flourishing in Sparta, declined. The restless, turbulent flood of creative effort which came out of Greece surged past Sparta on her militaristic island and left her high and dry. In the event, victory over Athens in the Peloponnesian war forced her to spread the Spartiate élite too thinly over subjugated areas. Her defeat by the Theban Epaminondas at Leuctra in 371 (largely through a novel oblique tactical approach, of immense future significance) left her no more than an archaic relic fading into obscurity.

In the city states of Hellas which had not chosen a military solution to their population problems, war was a tragic interruption in the life of the ordinary citizen.[6] It swept him into military service as a heavily armed infantryman if he were a man of substance, as a more lightly armed infantryman (a bowman perhaps, or a slinger) of less military significance if he were not. The obligation to serve under arms at need (and usually to furnish them) was an essential element in a man's standing as a free citizen,

Opposite: Bronze figure of a Greek heavy armed infantryman (a hoplite) from Dodona, c. 520 B.C. (Berlin)

13

Mythical battle of Greeks against Amazons (from the Mausoleum at Halicarnassus)

and it was not uncommon, as for instance in Athens with the *epheboi*, for young men to be required to establish their capacity to bear arms as a condition of full citizenship.

'The qualities of its courts of law and its armies,' said Goethe, 'give the most minute insight into the essence of an empire.'[7] The organization of these two fundamental types of social institution inevitably reflects the structure and outlook of the society they serve. Thus arrangements for military command in the armed forces of the πόλις in war largely reflect the approach to the distribution of political power in peace. In Athens, for example, at the beginning of the fifth century B.C., the time of the battle of Marathon, there were ten generals, elected by a show of hands in the assembly of the whole citizen body, the *ecclesia*. Unless this assembly also nominated one of them as commander-in-chief, at the start of a campaign, the στρατηγοί divided their functions. They presided each in turn for one day over their committee while they were in Athens. In the field, if more than one were present, each took it in turn to be commander-in-chief for a day.[8] The ταξίαρχοι, whom we might call colonels, were elected each in his tribe to command its infantry, assisted by λοχαγοί, or captains.

The elective principle for the appointment of officers appears again in the armies of the early Roman republic, and vestiges of it survive into imperial times. It was to be tried out centuries later in the American, French and Russian revolutionary armies, and was to be quickly abandoned in each. It only seems to have worked satisfactorily in the forces of relatively small political units using simple techniques of war, and even then only if what Aristotle would have recognized as democratic processes were characteristic of the parent society, which is not, of course, true of any sovereign nation state in the world today.

Military discipline among the lively and argumentative Athenians was none too good by any standard. It is characteristic that grosser breaches were only punished on the return of the expedition, after court cases which I imagine were often widely enjoyed. The typical Athenian hoplite, though paid a small wage and a subsistence allowance with another allowance for his attendant, and though he continued to be liable for military service from the time he was passed off as an *ephebus* at 20 until he was 60, remained essentially and always a civilian.

One of my early commanding officers said sadly to me, shortly after I went down from three or four years spent beside the infant Thames with polemarchs, hoplites and such, 'You'll never be a soldier: you'll never be much more than an armed civilian.' I felt, I must confess, rather chastened, but it did seem that I was in quite distinguished company.

With the Roman army it was different, and most strikingly so after the reforms of Marius in the early first century B.C.[9] Under the kings every citizen had been liable to serve in the army with such weapons as the grading of his property suggested he could afford. The richest class served as cavalry, the next as heavy infantry. The helmet, breastplate, greaves, metal shield and lance, furnished by the soldier himself, were costly. The four next lower classes in consequence served as more lightly armed infantry and the members of the lowest and poorest were often not required to serve at all. The introduction of pay resolved many of the objections to service from the poorer men, and Marius removed all property qualifications for service whatsoever.

By the middle of the second century B.C. (the time of Polybius), the legions were still raised, as required, from a general levy. Tribes were chosen by lot in turn and draftees from each tribe were nominated until the required number of legions was filled. There were even then old sweats known as *evocati* who regularly joined up without bothering to attend the drafting assembly. They were useful men and often became centurions.

Following pages: A Roman victory over barbarians (probably Dacians) in the third century A.D., the general (probably a portrait) in the middle. Chain mail and 'fish scale' armour are evident (Rome, National Museum)

Assault on a walled city, with scaling ladders (from a frieze of the Nereid Monument, fifth century B.C., found at Xanthos in Lycia)

Marius introduced a long-service regular army in which men enliste[d] for twenty years. He also reorganized the legion, now some 6,000 strong, into a more flexible arrangement of ten cohorts, each of something like battalion size and containing six centuries. The legion now received a standard – the eagle – and was soon, in Caesar's time, to be given a distinguishing number as well. This endowed it with a persistence as an entity which was previously lacking. Marshal Saxe was to propose in the mid-eighteenth century that regiments should be given a number, and no longer be known by the names of their colonels, with the same purpose.

Before long names were added to legionary numbers. When Augustus amalgamated his own and Anthony's armies after the battle of Actium in 31 B.C., there were sometimes two and in some instances even three legions with the same number. Those that were not disbanded were then distinguished by the addition of names to their numbers: III Augusta, III Cyrenaica, III Gallica. When new legions were raised later they too were given names.

The legion was now more than ever a continuing and coherent entity. The promotion of the centurion was largely within it, though cross posting from one legion to another on promotion was not uncommon. The loyalty of the soldier was at least in part engaged to it, though he had long since ceased to take an oath of allegiance to the general on enrolment and had from the time of Marius taken an oath to the republic instead, which was later to be replaced by an oath to the emperor. Legions developed distinguishable identities of their own, helped by their being stationed for long periods in the same districts with permanent quarters, the *castra stativa*, under *praefecti castrorum*. The XVII, XVIII and XIX legions, destroyed

Roman soldiery, both legionary and auxiliary, applying the 'testudo', or tortoise, formed of shields conjoined, to the assault of a fortified place (Trajan's Column, early second century A.D.: Trajan died in 117)

under Varus in Germany in A.D. 9, were never raised again. Nor was the IX Hispana, annihilated near Colchester by Britons under Boudicca in A.D. 61. The legion evoked some at least of the emotional associations of the modern regiment. Its solidity as a group strengthened even further, in battle, a soldiery who were already by temperament tough and obdurate and in whom the habit of obedience had been developed by a stern code of discipline.

Even those who admire the Romans most might hesitate to describe them as kindly folk. They were inclined to cruelty and expected it. The punishments inflicted on the soldier included death for desertion, mutiny or insubordination, and beating for stealing, false witness or culpable physical weakness. Public degradation was not unknown and the grimmer penalties were sometimes visited on whole units, decimated by the execution of one in ten (chosen by lot), or even killed off completely. In the palisade or turf wall of a legionary camp the front gate, the praetorian, was in the vicinity of the general's quarter and nearest the enemy. Half a mile or so behind it in the middle of the opposite side of the square was the *porta decumana*. 'Through this,' says Vegetius mournfully, 'guilty soldiers are

Decapitation of rebellious Germanic nobles in the wars of Marcus Aurelius (Aurelian Column, erected after the Emperor's death in A.D. 180). Humanity and anguish are more apparent in the philosopher-Emperor's memorial than in those of Trajan

19

conducted to their punishment . . .[10] Punishment and fear thereof are necessary to keep soldiers in order in quarters: but in the field,' Vegetius says, reflecting the sensible attitude of the Roman military in general, 'they are more influenced by hope and rewards.'[11]

In peacetime, however, the regime was severe. Tacitus recounts a story[12] of how Corbulo, in his efforts to strengthen discipline in the time of Claudius, had a soldier executed for working on field fortifications without wearing his sword, as the order prescribed, and another man because he had only a dagger. In the mutiny after the death of Augustus[13] the soldiers sought out and slew a centurion, old 'Cedo Alteram' or 'Give-Me-Another', who was called this because when he had broken his cane of office on a soldier's back he did not desist but demanded a replacement. And as a result the paternal relationship which sometimes existed between officer and man even in Frederick the Great's army, with its brutal and arbitrary discipline, can be sought in the imperial Roman army in vain. Paternalism in a social structure seems to be hardly possible without some sort of a gap between groups or strata, as between generations, for example, or social classes, or those on either side of an intellectual or educational barrier. It seems to depend upon an awareness of insecurity or inferiority on one side and of a secure superiority on the other. The Roman centurion, who acted as company commander and company sergeant-major in one, was a hard master. He came from the same level in society as his men.

Under the empire, while the practice that only Roman citizens should serve in the legions was continued, the disadvantages were realized of confining recruiting to Italians. Non-Italians were enrolled, therefore, and given the citizenship. Before long most legionary recruits came from the provinces. The praetorian and urban guard, however, continued to be found only among Italians.

The method of a centurion's promotion through the sixty centuries of the legion is still uncertain. The cohorts were numbered one to ten, and in each the six centuries followed a set order of precedence, with the same designation in each cohort.

It is possible that the steady old file who would never get far was promoted from one century to another through each of the ten cohorts in order, and if he started at the bottom would only become *primus pilus*, if he ever did, on his fifty-ninth promotion. More promising candidates (such as the young men of equestrian birth who had insufficient means to follow an equestrian public *cursus*) might be promoted up through the ten cohorts in one century, and on arrival in the first cohort go along through its six grades to the senior century of the legion. The *primus pilus*, the senior centurion (in the words of Vegetius), 'was not only entrusted with the eagle but commanded four centuries, that is 400 men in the first line. As head of the legion he had appointments of great honour and profit.[14]

The Roman legionary soldier of the late republic and the early empire was not a pure mercenary, if there is such a thing. He served for pay but though this was small he was rarely led astray by hope of plunder. Booty was divided out and was augmented by donatives. Caesar doubled the soldier's pay. It was then, according to my calculations, about the value in

Roman soldiery building fortifications, from Trajan's Column. The 'lorica segmentata' of the later first — and second — century equipment of the legionary here appears clearly in the central figures

1982 of £100 a year. But this is really meaningless. What seems to be the case is that though the Roman soldier had to buy his food (he was almost entirely vegetarian) he could live on his pay and even save, putting by a little money in the legionary savings bank, described by Vegetius,[15] for such purposes as the dignified funeral at which every good Roman citizen aimed.

But apart from the financial rewards he seemed to like a strictly ordered life. Dedication to the pursuit of arms came naturally to him. 'Their trade was war,' wrote the Earl of Orrery in his *Treatise of the Art of War* in 1677,[16] adding, 'I thank God ours is not.' A French officer of parachute troops operating in Algeria in 1960 said, 'We like war and we are tooled up for it.'[17] It could have been a Roman legionary soldier speaking.

The legionary machine was complex and highly articulated. The number and variety of titles of its junior officers is impressive.[18] Its weapons were primarily helmet, breastplate and shield, with a throwing spear (*pilum*), a sword of the Spanish type (*gladius*) and a dagger (*pugio*), but it also could call on some fairly sophisticated siege weapons.

Recruits under the late republic and the early empire were usually adequate in number and, because of the respectable social standing of a soldier's calling, of good average quality. Marriage was forbidden the soldier but allowed among officers. What very often happened was that the soldier lived with a woman who was recognized as his wife, and children were legitimized when he got his discharge.

Training was tough, realistic and rational. The Romans of the republic and the early empire took their army seriously. Men of education and position found in appointments as officers in it, especially those of tribune, a path to political advancement of which many of the abler and more ambitious took advantage. It is impossible not to be struck by the exactitude with which the Romans matched their personal characteristics, their social structure and their political organization with military institutions which most faithfully reflected them. This is not by any means the only example we shall meet of the reflection in military institutions of patterns in parent societies but it is one of the clearest.

When Vegetius wrote his account of the military institutions of the Romans[19] he was attempting to recall the citizens of the fourth century A.D. to the grim virtues and military skills of their ancestors. But the book, though perhaps the most influential of any military treatise between Roman times and the nineteenth century, and well worth reading today, had little influence in its own time. The decay which Vegetius laments in the military institutions of fourth century Rome was not confined to them and was itself only the symptom of a disease rather than the disease itself. The collapse of the Roman system during the following three centuries, under external pressures which internal tensions made it impossible to resist, carried the legionary system down along with it.

Before anything remotely resembling a legion was seen in Europe again, as a result of the military reforms of Maurice of Nassau 1,000 years later, feudalism was to develop and decline.

23

Ant exploiterent le
duc damou et fon
oſt quilz vindzen
deuant diuas. Et
quant ilz deurent approuchi

Knights
and Mercenaries

The military structure of mediaeval Europe was dominated by the castle and the heavily armoured mounted man-at-arms. These two could probably be described, in the terms we use today, as the two principal elements in one integral weapons system. It was essentially defensive. Feudal military service was highly regulated. The obligation to serve was to a person, under a contract clearly understood on both sides. A benefit was conferred (tenancy of land was by far the most common form of it) in return for which military service was required. The time to be served and the distance from home a man might have to travel on service were both small. In consequence extensive aggression was difficult to sustain. In the Hundred Years War England was only able to conquer a large part of France because the English king had feudal claims there. Crusading expeditions to the Near East demanded the invocation of quite exceptional sanctions.

The castle represented a heavy investment in labour and capital, but so, in other ways, did the knight. The arms and equipment (including the horse) of an armoured mounted soldier in twelfth-century France or England might represent the entire income for several years of a considerable little rural community.[20]

The military resources of a mediaeval monarch were determined by his position as a land-holder. The forces he could summon, even for the limited time in any year permitted by feudal custom, were often exceeded by those available to men who were his subjects, as for example the forces of the early Capet kings in France were outnumbered by those of the Dukes of Normandy. The permanent forces upon which a king could count were rarely more than modest.

The feudal mounted man-at-arms followed his calling primarily for the maintenance or improvement of the economic and social position of his family as a land-holding unit. Military service was one of the only two ways which were in practice open to him (the other being holy orders) for the acquisition of further wealth and prestige. For anyone not in holy orders, rank, dignity, administrative responsibility and the rewards thereof

Detail of the assault on Duras in the Hundred Years War. Both long and crossbows are here in use by the French (Froissart)

25

Clash of French and English knights at the Battle of Poitiers in the Hundred Years War, which was a clear victory for the English against heavy odds, largely through sensible use of ground and the effectiveness of the longbow, 19 September 1356

were all closely related to the extent of land held in fief. More extensive benefices could be expected to accrue to the distinguished performer in battle.

Plunder and ransom could also be expected to come the way of the mediaeval man-at-arms. The advantages, finally, of physical strength and skill at arms in the time of diminished public security which followed the collapse of Roman institutions need no emphasis.

The son of a knightly family, which held land in return for military service, was naturally brought up in the use of weapons and in hunting and robust physical sports more or less closely related to the practice of war. It would be less usual for him to learn to read and write. His principal weapons were the horse, the lance and a heavy sword (sometimes two-handed) with a choice of a variety of other minor cutting and stabbing weapons such as daggers and short swords, and of bruising and crushing weapons such as the club or mace. He wore a protective covering of leather and metal later partially extended to his horse. His dominance would have been impossible without the stirrup,[21] whose effect on European civilization ever since its introduction into Europe by Eurasian nomads has been enormous – almost certainly no less than that of printing or gunpowder.

Armour continued to be worn long after massed infantry and musketry had reduced the knight-at-arms to a figure of fantasy, a quixotic creature on an emaciated horse tilting at windmills. By the mid-sixteenth century armour was worn, if at all, more by princes than common soldiers, and not always by the most warlike princes at that.

Opposite: Surrender of Melun to Charles VII of France during his re-establishment of French royal control over English and rebel French forces, 1430–40

27

To judge by the museums, few princes possessed more suits of armour than Philip II of Spain (1556–98). Unlike his father Charles V he was rarely in battle.[22] Before long armour became rather like the scarlet tunics and bearskins of the Brigade of Guards in Britain: invaluable for ceremonial but offering fatal disadvantages in battle.

Missile weapons, such as the crossbow, were scarcely used by the mediaeval knight at all in war, though he frequently used them for hunting. The second Lateran Council in 1139 forbade the warlike use of the crossbow as a barbarous device, but its neglect by the mounted warrior sprang more from the real practical difficulty of using it from a horse.

The knight in the high Middle Ages, say for a century and a half on either side of 1300, fought as an individual. A twelfth-century battle developed almost as soon as it was joined into a number of individual engagements. Group skills found little place in feudal tactics. Field forces, too, were not large. From the eleventh century to the end of the fifteenth no reliable evidence exists of an army of more than 10–12,000 men. The army of Henry V of England at Agincourt in 1415 (where, contrary to a common belief, it was somewhat larger than the French[23]) was scarcely 6,000, the size of one Roman legion or the 1st British Airborne Division in the battle of Arnhem and half the size of the U.S. Pentomic Division of the late 1950s.

Embodied with the twelfth-century knight in a French or English feudal array were foot soldiers less well protected and in general more crudely armed (though using some missile weapons), who were themselves also discharging a personal obligation to give military service. Such interruptions to normal life were unwelcome but of short duration. The forces thus produced were usually cumbrous, ill-armed, and of low military value, though a sharp distinction must be made between these and foot soldiers

Crossbow, a highly worked specimen, probably intended for use by a great noble in hunting (Tower of London)

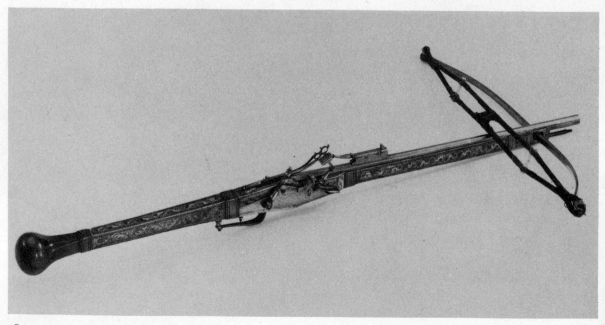

Above: Storming of Gergueau (Jargean, south-east of Orleans) by the French under Charles VII (Vigiles de Charles VII, Bibl. Nat. Fr. 5054)

Squire with a thick-bladed halberd and a crossbowman in battle order (Jouvencel and Froissart, Bibl. Nat. Fr.)

29

Opposite: One of the most celebrated suits of armour, that of General Erasmo Gattamelata, fifteenth century (Venice, Arsenal)

A crusading man-at-arms. The Cross of St George suggests this was a Genoese knight serving in the Holy Land (French, fourteenth century: Florence, Museo Nazionale)

English yeomen in
practice at the butts,
c.1340. Archery practice
was compulsory
throughout the land
(Loutrell Psalter)

found from free yeomen, like the English archers armed with the longbow, a weapon whose use had been learned in the Welsh wars. These were probably the most notable infantry on any European battlefield until the emergence of the Swiss, and unique in their kind.

It is perhaps just worth noting here, possibly for the benefit of some who think that what is of higher mechanical complexity must always be better than what is of less, that the crossbow was in almost every important respect a less efficient weapon than the longbow. That is to say, in accuracy, penetration, and rate of fire the longbow had the advantage all the way. Not till the nineteenth century were infantry to be equipped with anything offering a greater sum of advantages. The longbow's greatest drawback was the skill required for its effective use, which took years to acquire.

Jean Froissart, whose prose Chronicles *covered much of the history of fourteenth-century Europe, has been described by Geoffrey Brereton (whose admirable Penguin edition, first published in 1968, I have used here) as 'the first of the great war reporters'. Froissart was not so much the day-to-day journalist as the author of one of those great books put together after the event by correspondents, using the best contemporary material and their own personal experience. Much of Froissart's first book, from which extracts are given here, is based on the earlier chronicle of Le Bel, himself often an eyewitness.*

Froissart is no blind admirer of the knightly class which would furnish the greater part of his readership. In his account of the fighting in France in the Hundred Years War 'one's first impression is of crudely savage small wars and private feuds in emergent nations not far removed from tribalism', to quote Geoffrey Brereton. Nationality was still an imperfect concept, where large parts of France were held under the English crown, and members of the same family could turn up on different sides (and change them) as readily as in the American revolutionary war. A tradition of order and culture, of a sort, was to be found in the knightly class in western Europe but it was also capable of the massacre of prisoners and the public torture of enemies. Chivalry there was, but even more of self-interest. Edward III of England was only dissuaded from killing the whole citizenry of Calais, including the knights of the garrison, by the argument that this could rebound later on, in altered circumstances, upon his own people.

continued on page 41

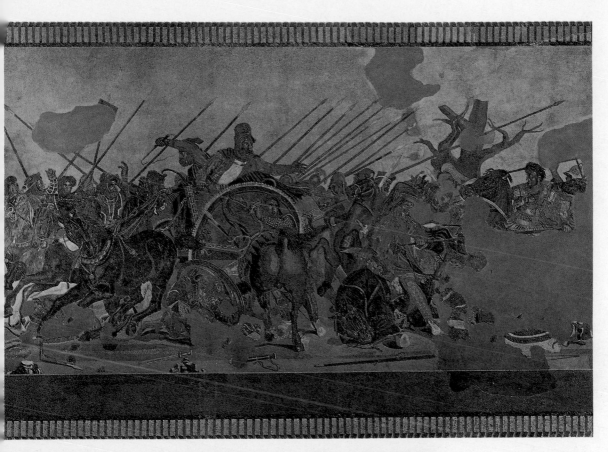

Above: Alexander the Great overcomes the Persians under Darius at the Battle of the Issus, 333 B.C., from a mosaic in the House of the Faun, Pompeii (Museo Nazionale, Naples)

Greek bronze helmet of the Corinthian type from Olympia. Inscription reads that it was dedicated to Zeus by the Argives as spoil taken from the Corinthians. Fifth century B.C. (British Museum)

33

The climax of the Iliad is
the single combat between
Achilles and Hector.
Achilles, with helmet,
shield and sheathed
sword, lunges forward to
deal a finishing stroke to
Hector, who is already
wounded and giving
ground. Detail of an Attic
Volute Krater, Red
Figure, c. 490 B.C.
Found at Cerveteri
(British Museum)

Left: Archaic
black-figure Greek vase
by the Exekias painter
c. 540 B.C. Achilles
slaying the Amazon
queen Penthesilea
(British Museum)

Right: Bronze statuette of a Roman legionary wearing a cuirass of overlapping bands of metal, joined front and back by leather thongs, over a leather doublet. This is the 'lorica segmentata', in general use in the second century A.D. *The fabric drawers adopted from auxiliaries and leather 'pterugae' hanging down from the doublet are also apparent (British Museum)*

Below: Greek mausoleum frieze from Halicarnassus. Mythical battle between Greek warriors and Amazons. Workshop of Skopas, c. *350* B.C. *(British Museum)*

Above: Alexander the Great (356–323 B.C.) assaults Tyre, as seen by a mediaeval artist. Landing-craft run inshore and men-at-arms attempt an escalade under a hail of stones and arrows. From a miniature in a French MS., Histoire du Grand Alexandre *(Petit Palais)*

Right: Battle of Crécy in the Hundred Years War. The French under Philip VI are totally defeated by the English under Edward III, 26 August 1346. The English longbow here confronts the French (or Genoese) crossbow. Chroniques de Froissart, *written late fourteenth century (Musée de L'Arsenal)*

Left: Warfare between Muslims and Christians is highlighted in this miniature from a thirteenth-century Spanish manuscript (Escorial Library)

Above: Entry into Florence of the army of Charles VIII in 1494 (Francesco Granacci, Florence, Palais Medici-Riccardi)

Defeat and death of Charles the Bold of Burgundy at the Battle of Nancy 1477 (from the Mémoires de Philippe de Commines, *Nantes, Musée Dobrée)*

*Philip II of Spain,
in armour, by
Titian (Prado,
Madrid)*

Right: Illumination from
the Berner Chronik of
Diebold Schilling
(Swiss: completed 1483)
showing soldiers armed
with hand-guns,
crossbows, halberds,
swords and spears

Left: Illumination in a manuscript of the works of
Quintus Curtius (completed 1468) showing
soldiers armed with hand-guns and cannon besieging
a castle (British Library)

continued from page 32

Froissart is here, in passages I have compressed but not otherwise altered, reporting in Book I on the campaign of Crécy in 1346. His vivid account throws a bright light on military practice in fourteenth-century Europe. What is reproduced here is especially relevant to the supremacy of the English archer on Western European battlefields and the superiority of the longbow, as a weapon, to the crossbow, so convincingly demonstrated once again at Agincourt in 1415. The campaign of 1346 was originally intended as a relief expedition into the province of Gascony, then part of the English realm but at that time under French pressure.

They made a good start towards Gascony, where the King intended to go. But the wind changed. The King held a new council at the suggestion of Sir Godfrey (Harcourt). 'Normandy,' said Sir Godfrey, 'is one of the richest countries in the world. I promise you, on my life, that once you reach it, it will be easy to land there. You will find large towns and fortresses completely undefended, in which your men will win enough wealth to make them rich for twenty years to come. Your fleet will be able to follow you almost as far as Caen. If you see fit to take my advice, you and all of us will profit by it. We shall have gold, silver, food supplies and everything else in abundance.'

The King ordered his seamen to change course for Normandy and entered La Hogue: the horses were unloaded from the ships with all the gear and a council was held to decide how they should proceed.

The men were divided into three columns, one to take the right flank and follow the coast, another the left, while the third marched in the centre under the King and the Prince of Wales. Each night the flanking columns led by the two Marshals were to join up again with the King.

The fleet sailed along the coast, seizing every vessel, large or small, that they fell in with. Archers and foot-soldiers marched near them within sight of the sea, robbing, pillaging and carrying off everything they came across. They moved forward by land and sea until they reached Barfleur, a seaport and fortified town which they took immediately because the inhabitants surrendered in the hope of saving their lives, though this did not prevent the town from being emptied of its gold, silver and jewelry. They found so much of it there that the very servants in the army turned up their noses at fur-lined gowns. All the men in the town were taken and put on board the ships so that there should be no danger of their rallying afterwards and harassing them in the rear.

After capturing and plundering Barfleur, though without burning it, they spread out over the country, though they still kept near the coast. They did whatever they pleased, for no one resisted them. They came in time to a large wealthy town and port called Cherbourg. They sacked and burnt part of it, but found the citadel too strongly defended to be taken, so they went on towards Montbourg and Valogne. This last they sacked completely and then set fire to it. They did the same to a number of other towns in the region, taking so much valuable booty that it would have been an impossible task to count it.

So was the good fat land of Normandy ravaged and burnt, plundered and pillaged by the English until the news of the havoc reached the King of France. The King summoned fighting men from every possible quarter and assembled one of the largest forces of great lords, dukes, counts, barons and knights that had been seen in France for a hundred years. But he had to bring them from such distant countries that it took a long time to collect them.

. . . On that day the English rose very early and made ready to advance. The King heard mass before sunrise, then mounted his horse, as did his son the Prince and Sir Godfrey of Harcourt, on whose advice the King largely relied. They moved forward in perfect order, with the Marshals' banner-bearers in the van, until they came close to the town of Caen and its defenders. These were waiting drawn up in the fields, apparently in excellent shape. But no sooner did the townsmen see the English advancing upon them in three solid, close-ordered divisions and catch sight of the banners and the innumerable pennons waving and fluttering in the wind and hear the shouting of the archers – all things of which they had had no previous experience – than they were so filled with dismay that nothing in the world could have stopped them taking to their heels. They turned and fled in confusion, in spite of everything the Constable could do. In a few moments their whole order of battle had broken up and they were rushing in terror to reach the safety of the town. Many of them stumbled and fell in the struggle to escape, while others piled on top of them in their panic.

The English [knights] were now among them killing as they liked without mercy. Meanwhile the English men-at-arms and archers were continuing the slaughter of the fugitives, sparing none. For three days the English remained in possession of Caen, where they won an amazing quantity of wealth for themselves. They used the time to put their forces in order and sent boats and barges laden with their gains – clothes, jewelry, gold and silver plate and many other valuable things down the river to where the main fleet lay.

So the King sent back his fleet full of conquered spoils and of good prisoners, including more than sixty knights and three hundred wealthy citizens, with a host of loving greetings to his wife, the gracious Queen of England. King Philip was eager to come up with the English and engage them. At about noon he reached Airaines, which the King of England had quitted in the early morning. The French found that large quantities of provisions had been left behind. There was meat on the spits, there were loaves and pies in the ovens, barrels and kegs of wine, and many tables ready laid, for the English had left in great haste.

. . . The King [of England] gave orders for the whole army to be armed and ready to move on again at the sound of the trumpets. He slept little that night, but rose at midnight and had the trumpeters sound a signal to strike camp. Soon everything was ready, the pack horses loaded and the waggons filled. By sunrise they were near to the ford (across the Somme). But the tide was in and they could not cross, so the King was obliged to wait for the rest of his men to catch up with him. By that time, the knight whom King Philip had sent to guard the crossing had appeared on the opposite bank with a thousand men-at-arms and five thousand foot-soldiers, including the Genoese. This brought no change to the King of England's plans. He ordered his Marshals to strike at once into the water and his archers to shoot steadily at the French opposite.

The bravest knights hurled their horses into the water, with the best mounted in the lead. There were many jousts in the river and many unhorsings on both sides, for Sir Godemar and his men defended the crossing bravely. A number of his knights, with others from Artois and Picardy, had decided not to wait on the bank but to ride into the ford and fight there in order to win greater distinction. So there was many a joust and many a skilled piece of fighting, for the knights sent to defend the shallows were picked men who stood in good order at the neck of the crossing and clashed fiercely with the English as these came up out of the water. The Genoese also did much damage with their crossbows, but the English archers shot so well together that it was an amazing sight to see. And while they were harassing the French, the mounted men got through.

When the English had scattered the enemy and cleared the ground, they formed up in excellent order, assembled their supply-train and moved off in their habitual way. Early the next day the King struck camp and moved towards Crécy. The King encamped in the open fields with his army and since he was willing to risk the fortunes of battles with numbers which he knew were only an eighth of those of the King of France, he had to give urgent thought to his dispositions.

So King Edward stood down his men for the day, with orders to assemble early next morning at the sound of the trumpets, in readiness to fight at once on the chosen positions. They all went to their quarters and busied themselves in checking and polishing their arms and armour.

He rose fairly early in the morning and heard mass with his son the Prince of Wales.

The King then gave orders for every man to go to the positions decided upon the day before. Close to a wood in the rear he had a large park set up, in which all the wagons and carts were put. All the horses were led into this park, leaving every man-at-arms and archer on foot. The park had only one entrance.

He caused his Constable and his Marshals to divide the army into three bodies. In the first was his son the young prince.

Returning to his own division, he gave orders for all the men to stand down and eat and drink at their ease. Having done this and packed up the pots, kegs and provisions in the carts again, they went back to their battle-positions. They sat down on the ground with

The English capture Caen from the French in 1346 in the Hundred Years War (Froissart)

their helmets and bows in front of them, so as to be fresh and rested when the enemy arrived.

The King rode slowly round the ranks escorted by his Marshals, encouraging his men. He spoke to them in such a smiling, cheerful way that the most disheartened would have plucked up courage on hearing him.

The King of France sent forward four gallant knights, who approached so near to the English that they obtained a very good view of their dispositions. The English saw clearly what they were doing, but made no move but let them ride off unmolested. The four returned towards the King of France and his commanders, who had been walking their horses until they came back and halted when they saw them. The King commanded one of the bravest and most chivalrous of knights and one of the most experienced in war and commanded him to give his opinion.

'Sire', said he, 'we viewed the English lines. They are drawn up in three divisions, very prettily disposed and show no sign of intending to retreat. They are obviously waiting for you. You should halt all your men now and encamp in the open for today. Before the rear can come up with you it will be getting late. Your men will be tired and you will find that the enemy are fresh and rested and in no doubt of the way they plan to fight. In the morning you will be able to see which is the best line of attack. You can be sure that they will still be there.'

The King approved this advice and ordered his Marshals to put it into execution. The leaders halted but those behind continued to advance. So pride and vanity took charge of events. Neither the King nor his Marshals could restrain them any longer, for there were too many great lords among them, all determined to show their power.

They rode on in this way, in no order or formation, until they came within sight of the enemy. For what they did then the leaders were much to blame. As soon as they saw the English they reined back like one man, in such disorder that those behind were taken by surprise and imagined they had already been engaged and were retreating. Yet they still had room to advance if they wished to. Some did, while others stopped where they were.

The English, who were drawn up in their three divisions and sitting quietly on the ground, got up with perfect discipline when they saw the French approaching and formed their ranks, with the archers in harrow-formation and the men-at-arms behind.

French lords – kings, dukes, counts and barons – did not reach the spot together, but arrived one after another, in no kind of order. When King Philip came near the place where the English were and saw them, his blood boiled, for he hated them. Nothing could now stop him from giving battle. He said to his Marshals: 'Send forward our Genoese and begin the battle, in the name of God and St Denis.'

He had with him about fifteen thousand Genoese bowmen who would sooner have gone to the devil than fight at that moment, for they had just marched over eighteen miles, in armour and carrying their crossbows. They told their commanders that they were not in a state to fight much of a battle just then.

While this argument was going on and the Genoese were hanging back, a heavy storm of rain came on and there were loud claps of thunder, with lightning.

Then the sky began to clear and the sun shone out brightly. But the French had it straight in their eyes and the English at their backs. The Genoese, having been marshalled into proper order and made to advance, began to utter loud whoops to frighten the English. The English waited in silence and did not stir. The Genoese hulloa'd a second time and advanced a little farther, but the English still made no move. Then they raised a third shout, very loud and clear, levelled their crossbows and began to shoot.

At this the English archers took one pace forward and poured out their arrows on the Genoese so thickly and evenly that they fell like snow. When they felt those arrows piercing their arms, their heads, their faces, the Genoese, who had never met such archers before, were thrown into confusion. Many cut their bowstrings and some threw down their crossbows. They began to fall back.

46

Opposite: The English
storm Calais in 1347
(Froissart)

Left figure: An English
longbowman of the
Hundred Years War

Right figure: French
knight of the eleventh
century (Dialogue of St
Gregory: Bibl. Nat.
Fr.)

Below: Fighting in the
Hundred Years War
(Froissart)

Between them and the main body of the French there was a hedge of knights, splendidly mounted and armed, who had been watching their discomfiture and now cut off their retreat. For the King of France, seeing how miserably they had performed, called out in great anger: 'Quick now, kill all that rabble. They are only getting in our way!' Thereupon the mounted men began to strike out at them on all sides and many staggered and fell, never to rise again. The English continued to shoot into the thickest part of the crowd, wasting none of their arrows. They impaled or wounded horses and riders, who fell to the ground in great distress, unable to get up again without the help of several men.

So began the battle between La Broye and Crécy in Ponthieu at four o'clock on that Saturday afternoon.

The King of France was in great distress when he saw his army being destroyed piecemeal by such a handful of men as the English were. He asked the opinion of Sir John of Hainault, who was at his side. 'Well, Sire,' Sir John answered, 'the only advice I can give you now is to withdraw to some place of safety, for I see no hope of recovery. Also, it will soon be dark and you might just as easily fall in with your enemies and meet disaster as find yourself among friends.'

The King, shaking with anger and vexation, made no immediate reply, but rode on a little farther as though to reach his brother the Count of Alençon, whose banners he could see at the top of a small rise. The Count was launching a very well-ordered attack on the English, as was the Count of Flanders from another quarter. They moved their forces along the flank of the archers and reached the Prince of Wales's division, which they engaged fiercely for a long time. King Philip would gladly have joined them had it been possible, but there was such a throng of archers and men-at-arms in front of him that he could not get through. The farther he advanced, the smaller his numbers grew . . .

The lateness of the hour harmed the French cause as much as anything, for in the dark many of the men-at-arms lost their leaders and wandered about the field in disorder only to fall in with the English, who quickly overwhelmed and killed them. They took no prisoners and asked no ransoms, acting as they had decided among themselves in the morning when they were aware of the huge numbers of the enemy.

Yet some French knights and squires, and with them Germans and Savoyards, succeeded in breaking through the Prince of Wales's archers and engaging the men-at-arms in hand-to-hand combat with swords. There was much brave and skilful fighting. All the flower of the English knighthood was there with the Prince.

If the English had mounted a pursuit they would have accounted for many more, including the King himself. But this did not happen. On the Saturday they never once left their positions to pursue the enemy but stayed to defend themselves against attack.

Where in the Middle Ages land was scarce and offspring many, military expeditions might originate which were not entirely dominated by the concept of liege service. The crusades were of this sort, though liege service certainly played a large part in them, both in the expeditionary forces themselves and in the structure of occupation forces in the overseas colonies they established. Spirited adventurers also sought their fortune with their swords, singly or in groups, with no pretence of service to anything but their own interests, as several of the sons of Tancred de Hauteville did when they descended on southern Italy from Normandy in a Norman Conquest preceding that of England by half a century, and scarcely less important in its consequences. Individual free enterprise, related to but outside the framework of liege service, becomes more important as time goes by. The Western European mercenary begins to emerge.

The treaty of Brétigny between England and France in 1360, bringing to an end one distinct phase of the almost endless warfare between them, left hosts of soldiers unemployed, of whom many found their way down into Italy. The scourge of marauding armed bands under an elected leader was known elsewhere in Europe. It was only in Italy that the companies of fortune, as these were sometimes called, played an important political role.[24]

The city states of northern Italy in the fourteenth century were seeking a form of military organization appropriate to their needs, in circumstances of almost continuous conflict, in which the feudal contract of military service for land tenure had largely ceased to function. The form they settled on was the use of hired professionals. These were raised under a contract, or *condotta*, by a military contractor, a *condottiere*, who was paid by the state which hired him and was responsible on his side for the production of an adequately equipped and trained force and, as a rule, its command in the

field. Gian Galeazzo Visconti, for instance, first hereditary Duke of Milan, depended for his military successes upon the mercenary army led by Façino Cane. With it he took Vicenza and Padua from Venice and threatened the safety of Florence, defended by the famous English *condottiere* Sir John Hawkwood.

Ready cash was plentiful in the Italian cities of the *Trecento*, the 'thirteen hundreds', or what we call the fourteenth century, in which the development of a money economy was far advanced. There was plenty of human material as well. Landless men, incapable of craftsmanship or unwilling to work as craftsmen, abounded.

The Swiss cantons allowed recruiting and even sold recruits. From Germany a ferocious and disorderly soldiery, both mounted and dismounted, the *Reiter* and the *Landsknechte*, were readily enrolled.

The first fifty years of the fifteenth century in Italy, even more than the closing decades of the fourteenth, throw an interesting light on purely mercenary warfare. By 1421 Milan, under the Visconti, had acquired with the aid of the mercenary general Carmagnola a dominant position in the north. Venice bought Carmagnola away. He was replaced in Milan by an even more able and famous soldier of fortune, Francesco Sforza, son of a *condottiere* from the Romagna and a person of huge vigour and high ability. Carmagnola was no match for Sforza. The Venetian fleet was destroyed. Carmagnola was recalled to Venice and publicly executed. Sforza survived the attacks of the Venetians to become master of Milan and its new duke.

51

The search for security through purely mercenary troops, owing no political loyalty and without personal ties to the city they served, often brought greater evils in its train than those it avoided. The system was to be passionately attacked by Machiavelli, as we shall see. It is not surprising that occasional efforts were made by the cities to tie the captains more closely to them. Hawkwood was offered in Florence something like a permanent *condotta*, a contract for life. The same city later offered Count Conrad von Eichelberg the same sort of arrangement. Milan too was feeling its way towards some more enduring system of contract. All the cities found that troops recruited locally by a native *condottiere* were likely to be more reliable than foreign mercenaries under foreign captains.

The problem of how to establish effective control by the body politic over its own armed forces was still to be solved. Even the execution of Carmagnola by the Venetians did no more than emphasize the difficulty of finding a solution. It was still unsolved when northern Italy ceased to be an arena for conflict between rival Italian city states and became instead a battleground for foreign powers.

The motives of the *condottieri* and their men seem obvious enough; but whatever the reasons are for which a man will allow himself to be killed, or to be put in serious risk of it, money is not often high among them. A man will suffer great inconvenience and hardship for pay, and inflict a great deal more of it on other people. Men have often been known to kill others for money, but the cases where they will sell their own lives for cash alone are, I imagine, exceedingly rare. A soldier who stands by his contract and thinks he is nothing but a mercenary may find his motives, if he examines them, more complicated. The good fighting man who honestly believes himself to be a pure mercenary in arms, doing it all for the money, may have to guard his convictions as vigilantly as any atheist.

Certainly the cash inducement was clearly insufficient to cause men freely to give up their lives in the *Quattrocento*. Machiavelli wrote savagely of mercenary companies of horse. 'They are disunited, ambitious, without discipline, faithless, bold amongst friends, cowardly amongst enemies, they have no fear of God, and keep no faith with men.'[25] The soldiers were the *condottiere*'s working capital and he did not want to waste them. As for the soldiers: 'They have no love or other motive to keep them in the field beyond a trifling wage, which is not enough to make them ready to die for you.'

Battles in fifteenth-century Italy might be protracted but they were often almost bloodless as well. In the battle of Zagonara, a victory 'famous throughout all Italy', says Machiavelli, 'none were killed excepting Lodovico degli Obizzi, and he together with two of his men was thrown from his horse and suffocated in the mud'.

Machiavelli attacked the mercenaries because he saw that the Italian cities had made a serious error, an error which was in fact to prove fatal. He realized the intimate connection between military techniques and political methods, between military organizations and political institutions. He saw that the cities, whose competitive development was bound to lead to conflict, had completely failed to evolve military forms appropriate to their

The Arte of warre,
written first in Italiã
by *Nicholas Machiauell*, and set
forthe in Englishe by Peter
Whitehorne, studient at Graies Inne:
with an addiciõ of other like mar-
tialle featrs and experimen-
tes, as in a Table in the
ende of the Booke
maie appere.

Anno . M . D . L X .
Menß Iulij.

A Flemish picture of incidents in the Battle of Pavia, fought in 1525 by the King of Spain, about to become the Emperor in 1530 as Charles V, against the French. In this picture the extraordinary complexity of the politico-military scene in renaissance Italy is apparent. It could almost be Washington in the 1980s (Naples, Capodimonte)

political structure. He went even further and indicted them for failing to regard the political and military spheres as one organic whole in which political institutions cannot be shaped in disregard of their military implications without disastrous results. Machiavelli dreamed of an Italy united under Florence, and in looking for a suitable military form it was almost inevitable that he should turn to Rome.

The invincibility of the citizen army of the Roman republic was proof to Machiavelli of the rational nature of its organization. In his study of it he followed Vegetius. He probably went further than any predecessor, however, in his analysis of the general nature of war. He saw war as total and all embracing. The whole resources of the state should be applied to it and the only criterion of warlike methods should be their effectiveness. A decision could only come from battle 'which is the end for which all armies are raised'. The aim was victory and subjugation. Machiavelli was in some important respects a forerunner of Clausewitz. It is not surprising that Clausewitz admired him greatly.

Before long there were to be military developments which would give a new direction to human affairs. But though the military revolution which would shortly follow owed something to the inspiration of the Roman legion, it led in quite a different direction from any indicated by Machiavelli. This all began with the introduction of firearms.

The first significant effect of firearms was not to increase fire power on the battlefield but to destroy the immunity of fortresses. This was effectively demonstrated by Charles VIII's invasion of Italy, at the time of

Another aspect of the Battle of Pavia. Few people got badly hurt in battles such as this

The fifteenth-century hand-gun, or 'fire stick' (From a tapestry in Notre Dame de Nantilly, Saumur)

the arrival in the Americas of the Genoese captain in Spanish service, Christopher Columbus, in 1494. Independently of the introduction of firearms, however, another and at the time no less important change took place: the replacement of massed heavy cavalry as the decisive element on the European battlefield by massed heavy infantry. The pikemen of the Swiss squares, already long feared, shattered the chivalry of Burgundy at Nancy in 1477, where Charles the Bold died, seventeen years before the expedition of Charles VIII into Italy which first brought mobile artillery effectively into action against fortification.

The combination of missile effect and mobility in the joint action of longbowman and mounted man-at-arms, which had seen perhaps its most striking demonstration at Agincourt, was no longer an option. Cavalry could not easily be brought to charge home against a porcupine of pikes.[26] Armed with a wheel-lock pistol in the early sixteenth century the cavalry trooper in the attack was little better off than the pike-trailing infantryman in the defence. Sixteen feet was thought a suitable length for the pike. 'Few ordinary ammunition pistols,' said Lord Orrery, as late as 1677, 'do certain execution much farther off.'[27]

Hand firearms were in use at least as early as 1364,[28] but they were little more than metal tubes mounted on sticks. They were far less efficient than crossbow or longbow and were often only effective at close quarters (as is suggested, for instance, in some tapestries) when used as clubs. The longbow, in rapidity of fire, penetration and accuracy was so much superior not only to the crossbow but also to any hand firearm that a plea was raised in England as late as the mid-seventeenth century for its

King Gustavus Adolphus of Sweden at the critical Battle of Lutzen, 1632, in the Thirty Years War (1618–48)

reintroduction.[29] The firearm had come to stay, however, if only because it was so inaccurate that there was nothing but a waste of time in trying to train marksmen with it. Bowmen were skilled men. Arquebus men were not. Unskilled soldiery were easily come by and maintained. But firearms were also very frightening and their morale effect alone would have been quite sufficient to ensure their development.

The effort to find a tactical organization in which fire power and infantry shock tactics could be combined led to the major innovations of Maurice of Nassau at the beginning of the seventeenth century. He, too, turned back to the Roman legion, away from the mass of the Swiss square or the scarcely less massive Spanish *tercio*, to a linear formation, in two or three lines, articulated into units of about battalion size.

This time the return to the Roman model dreamt of by Machiavelli came off. Gustavus Adolphus, with new weapons, successfully developed and applied it on the battlefield, and the system he evolved persisted in its essentials well into the twentieth century. Units were smaller. Tactical deployment and adjustment were easier. A new requirement began to develop for initiative in junior leaders, of whom more were now needed.

Cavalry were released from the profitless pursuit of the *caracole*, advancing to the enemy at a trot and discharging their pistols. They could now apply true shock action. Drill and exercise for the infantry ceased to be merely a means to physical and moral health and became the basis of tactics. Precision in movement demanded marching in step. The group subordination of a living organism which was neither the immobile mass of heavy infantry nor the collection of bellicose individuals of the feudal array demanded better discipline and a more closely coherent whole. Military uniforms would not now be long in coming.

New possibilities for the use of armies were opened up by the restless genius of Gustavus Adolphus. A strategy of extensive operations was now possible. Armies grew in size. Military administration made new demands upon governments. The nature of the soldier's contract soon came under review.

The armies of the wars of religion in the sixteenth and seventeenth centuries were largely made up of part-time mercenaries. It was not necessarily the case that only a mercenary army was capable of operating under the Maurician system, though it had advantages for the purpose. The mercenary soldier minded little how far he campaigned from home or for how long. Recruiting through captains saved governments a good deal of trouble. The required standard of discipline and training was more easily produced.

The great victories of Gustavus Adolphus of Sweden were won by a conscript national militia, and not by full-time regular mercenaries, it is true, but in Sweden the social pattern was unusual. Sweden had never been completely feudalized and had never known the general domination of the mounted man-at-arms. Serfdom was non-existent and peasant proprietors were plentiful. The military strength of the country lay in its infantry: a conscript militia was in Sweden both a political and a military possibility.

In other parts of Europe it was thought that only a mercenary system would work, and in these a mercenary army became by the early seventeenth century the normal type of land force. But even before the end of the sixteenth century the disbandment of regiments at the end of one campaigning season and their re-raising at the start of the next, hitherto a general practice, was seen to be an inefficient and costly way of furnishing the state with soldiers. The practice spread of retaining troops in service throughout the year. Regular standing armies were before long to be the rule. But as Professor Roberts has pointed out, the permanent embodiment of armies which developed in this time was the result of military rather than political considerations.[30] A standing army developed not because growing royal absolutism depended upon it, nor because kings had to find employment for privileged or troublesome upper classes. It was the result of a military requirement.

Now that armies were permanently embodied it was not long before they came directly under a sovereign's control, raised, paid, in some respects equipped, and in part housed directly by him. 'Once the armies became royal (as the navies already were),' says Professor Roberts, 'the way was open for their eventually becoming national.'

Armies
of the Nation State

The development of armies as long-service, whole-time, regular forces under the sole control of the national authority, what I describe as their regularization, was a feature of the stabilization of the pattern of sovereign states in Western Europe. It can be seen very clearly in France between the time of Charles VII, when a nation in arms under royal leadership ejected the English, and the French Revolution, when a regular royal army proved quite incapable of saving the monarchy from the nation. From the time of Condé's victory over the Spanish army at Rocroi in 1643 the French army led the fashion in European standing armies for a century. Let us look at military developments in seventeenth-century France a little more closely.

Very noticeable is the rise in numbers.[31] Henry VI at the beginning of the century had an army of some 15,000, of whom 3,000 were Swiss. The Thirty Years War, which lasted from 1618 to 1648 right across the middle of the century, saw a large increase. The French army of 1678 numbered some 280,000 men. In the wars of Louis XIV numbers still further increased. There were 440,000 men on the strength in 1690, in a population of little more than 20 million. This represents an unusually high proportion of the male population under arms, the military participation ratio,[32] as it has been called, or M.P.R. After each peace, numbers naturally declined. In the less turbulent decades after 1713 they fell below 130,000. The general trend, however, is upward. It had become common in the mid-seventeenth century to keep 160–200,000 men under arms even in peace – twelve times as many as at the end of the sixteenth century.

An acute and dedicated investigator of military patterns in France, A. Babeau, writing in the nineteenth century, sees an image of the French people in the structure of the mid-seventeenth-century French army.[33]

At the bottom are the lowest orders, the valets, carters in the field and labourers for the engineers, who were not allowed to enlist as soldiers. Then came the mass of infantry soldiers, the main body of the nation; then the junior officers, the bourgeoisie; then the higher commanders, the nobility; at the top the king.

Thirty Years War: the Sack of Magdeburg by Tilly in 1631

Following pages: The taking of Thionville on 8 August 1645 by the Duc d'Enghien, the Great Condé, following up his great victory over the Spanish at Rocroi in 1643, when he was twenty-seven years old

Chivalry ceases finally to be a source of military strength in France with the disappearance of the *arrière ban*, the feudal array of the lesser nobility. From 1695, by which time military rank had become distinct from social, the part played by the French noble in military affairs is that of an officer in a regiment.

It is curious that even in a time of almost total absolutism, under Louis XIV, the French regular army was raised by voluntary enlistment. It continued to be raised thus until the Revolution. Louvois established a forced militia service in 1689 which aroused profound and enduring repulsion among the peasantry. Militia service was considered degrading; professional armed service was not. Even an army of 300,000 in a population of 20 million could still be raised by voluntary enlistment, and though not only prestige and promises but even ruses and force were sometimes used to bring men in, general conscription was not. It needed a revolution under the watchwords of liberty, equality and fraternity, threatened by foreign arms and internal sedition, to bring back forced general military service in the *levée en masse* of 1793, and to ensure the pitiless repression of all opposition to it in the massacres in La Vendée.

The fact was that a large reservoir of rough and restless manpower existed in France after the peace of Westphalia which in 1648 brought the Thirty Years War to an end. The idle and the ne'er-do-well abounded. Paupers were plentiful. The captains were personally responsible for keeping up the strength of their companies and the initial sum paid to a man on enrolment was their chief instrument of persuasion. Bigger recruits cost more and cavalrymen were dearer than foot soldiers. You could get a man for the infantry, not much above the minimum height of 5 ft to 5 ft 3 ins, for 100 livres in the mid-seventeenth century. In 1731 you might pay twice as much, and a fine big fellow of 5 ft 7 ins was known to cost 600. There

Plunder of a village in the Thirty Years War (From an etching of 1633 by Jacques Callot. Bibl. Nat. Fr.)

ere, as you might expect, complaints that rich cavalry officers spoilt the market by paying too much.

The average age of recruits was 20 to 30 years and 16 the lowest at which they were generally accepted. In the time of Louis XIII the engagement appears to have been for at least six months. As the military advantages of longer service became clearer the term increased. It was three years under Louis XIV, then four. Under Louis XV it increased to six and then eight. As gentler manners became more widespread in the eighteenth century many real recruiting abuses dropped away, but as times grew more settled and the general standard of living rose, recruits were harder to find. Not all soldiers were released on completion of their contract. An engagement for six years could easily let a man in for twelve. Abuses such as these lessened as the century wore on. The ordinances of 1788 removed many of the last. Institutions often approach their peak of excellence when they are about to disappear. The army of the *ancien régime* was one such.

Before 1778 there was no medical examination for entry into the French service, which made it easier for women to join. There had never, in fact, been much curiosity about a recruit's past and until the mid-eighteenth century only perfunctory enquiry as to his identity. He would nearly always take another name on joining, anyway, a *nom de guerre*, according to a practice almost universal in France from the sixteenth century to the Revolution. Beauvisage, Belhomme, Belamy, Joli-Coeur, could be found in many regiments. There were also La Jeunesse, Bon-Vivant and Belle-Humeur, with Vive l'Amour, Prêt-à-Boire and names of martial air like Sans-Quartier, Pied-Ferme or Frappe d'Abord. Napoleon's Marshal Victor, Duke of Belluno, got his name of Beau-Soleil in this way.

A soldier only lost his *nom de guerre* if he were disgraced, when his comrades would not use it any more. When the Free French in the Second

The miserable lot of soldiers when the war is over (J. Callot)

Pay day for the army, 1716 (Bibl. Nat. Fr.)

World War took on *noms de guerre*, usually to avoid inconvenience to families still in France, many in other national armies were surprised at the ease with which their companions accepted and used them. This was, however, a custom rooted in the pre-Revolutionary French military tradition and reflected in our own time in the Foreign Legion.

The French soldier of the *ancien régime* was not badly paid. He was also reasonably fed. The daily ration of one-and-a-half pounds of munition bread which the French soldier was drawing at the end of the nineteenth century was established nearly 200 years before. The regulation also prescribed a pound of meat a day and the soldier sometimes got it. He fed better than the peasant, for he ate more meat. This was a very important element in a system of voluntary recruiting.

Up to the late seventeenth century soldiers were mostly lodged in garrison towns, in pairs among civilian households. They were usually idle, often drunk and nearly always a nuisance in a small dwelling where there might be daughters. Barracks were built, usually in frontier districts to begin with, towards the end of the seventeenth century. The burghers were relieved but the soldier lost his freedom. After his day's work he was no longer his own master, until (if he were not on guard) the *appel du tambour*. Cavalry units were known to have been compelled to pay for improvements to their uniform on the threat of being removed from village billets if they did not. In barracks, ill-lit and unhygienic, three beds occupied 20 sq. ft. Each was 4 ft wide and three men slept in it.

Until the mid-seventeenth century the only clothing the king provided was shoes. Foreign troops in French service were the first to be completely uniformed. Louvois wanted to introduce uniform for French trops in 1668 but the captains protested they could not afford it. By the end of the century, however, as was also the case by then in England, uniform was general: white for the French infantry, blue for the German regiments in French service, red for the Irish and Swiss. The cockade was worn from 1710, but was only white from 1767.

Discipline was generally strict but its level of severity varied greatly. So long as the captains were responsible for recruiting and maintenance the men were treated on the whole quite gently.

In camp (J. Callot)

In 1762, in France, Choiseul took away the ownership of companies. The soldier was given a more august authority to which he might appeal, but it was also more distant and less personal. Discipline became stricter, more uniform, less paternal. The reign of Louis XV (1715–74) saw reforms which increased the efficiency of the army but were often harmful to the soldier's condition. Before then the men were less well exercised but more contented. In the early eighteenth century it took several hours to form a line of cavalry and no general dared set a large number of squadrons in motion. After the reforms of Louis XV it was said that cavalry exercises were more exactly performed but the horses broke down more frequently.

On the whole, however, morale remained high and there was a considerable degree of understanding between officers and men, as a Dr Moore reported in *A View of Society and Manners in France*, published in London in 1786. Everywhere it became more strained as the Revolution approached.

Women followed the armies in considerable numbers. Under Louis XIII a provision of four trollops per 100 men was thought to be a prudent way of protecting the womenfolk of the countryside. Wives and children also moved around. In 1718 it was reported that though there were no married men in some companies, others had forty or fifty. In 1772 it was said that the women gave more trouble than four times the same number of soldiers.

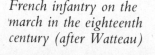

French infantry on the march in the eighteenth century (after Watteau)

Vivandières as seen in 1859

Permission to marry was often refused, though occasionally senior officers thought a small number of wives was useful. They did some cooking, washing and nursing. Whatever efforts were made to keep them away there were always a few wives around a regiment, and some dogs.

The French soldier was volatile, resilient, gay. He ran away readily in battle but also attacked with a fierce *élan*, going to his death, it was said in Italy in Louis XIII's time, as though he expected resurrection on the morrow. He was often, until the eighteenth century brought in milder ways, savage to the defeated. Prisoners, if there was little chance of getting them ransomed according to recognized scales and they would not change sides (which they often did), were sometimes simply killed.

Violent pillage, though common up to the seventeenth century, was rare after the time of Louis XIV. It remained common practice, however, to strip the dead of clothing and jewellery. 'My friends,' said a colonel, showing the well-dressed enemy to his regiment in rags, 'go and clothe yourselves.'

At the end of the seventeenth century billeting was the rule and quartering in barracks the exception. At the end of the eighteenth the reverse was true. Until the time of Louis XIV the soldier wore on his person, except for the shoes he had from the king, only the clothing he brought with him. Thereafter he wore a uniform furnished by his employer. These two developments, barrack life and the wearing of

Following pages: Prussian uniforms in 1786

69

Gaming before Troy: Ajax and Achilles (Attic Amphora, late sixth century B.C., *Vatican Museum)*

uniform, have probably done more to set the soldier apart in society than anything else.

Probably the special nature of the soldier's contract and the importance of group identifications in armed forces suggest that a threshold between the civil and military ways of life is inevitable. How much of this now remains? Will the military life lose something important if we try to bring about its total disappearance?

The Spartiate might sleep at home where his wife lived, but never dine there. He had always to eat in the common mess. At the other extreme is the concept of an army as just another occupational group in an industrial society. An undergraduate perhaps had something of the sort in mind recently, when he wrote that he now saw he had been mistaken about the army: he realized that it was in fact 'a competitive nine-to-five industry'. He meant, of course, competing for his own services, but even then he was mistaken. An army is not an industry and its members cannot be regarded industrial workers, with the pattern of their activities, and their rewards, determined by the practices of the market place.

Some of the big military operators in the United States in the Second World War thought that the invasion of Europe was no more than just another large-scale engineering project and declared their intention to treat it as such. I shall have more to say about the American experience in armed service later on and will only put in here that to think in this way is to ignore what, more than anything else, sets the military apart from most other groups – what I call the unlimited liability clause in a soldier's contract. When men are unprepared for this, and it is invoked, the results can be disturbing. The nature of his contract sets the man-at-arms apart. But how far apart? That is an important question today. I shall return to this and consider at the same time the intrusion of industrial and business management techniques into military practice.

I leave the French soldier of the mid-eighteenth century with regret, some whiskered musketeer inappropriately named La Violette, perhaps, or Perce Neige, sitting in his insanitary barracks – that 'honourable prison' – wondering possibly what to do with his time. With seven hours for sleep, one for meals, two for rest and four for exercises he has ten hours of free time and must spend most of it in barracks. Perhaps he is reflecting on how to prolong the life of his uniform, for it is expected to last three years and in order to do so must be kept two-thirds of the time unused. Perhaps he is doing another man's hair for him, using some of the cleaning and toilet kit which takes up so much of his carrying capacity in the field. Perhaps he is brooding over the growing severity of the exercise and the strictness of a discipline which has com in, like the new military hair fashions, from Prussia.

The Prussian military system and its influence in Europe in the second half of the eighteenth century, the nature of warfare in the age of the Enlightenment, its rude disturbance by the Napoleonic wars and the professionalization of the profession of arms which followed is what I shall deal with next.

BATAILLE D'AUSTERLITZ.
2 Decembre 1805.

Prussia
and Napoleon

The peace of Westphalia in 1648 at the end of the Thirty Years War brought more or less to an end a period in which fervent Christians were prepared to hang, burn, torture, shoot or poison other fervent Christians with whom they happened to disagree upon the correct approach to eternal life. The next eighty years, up to the mid-eighteenth century, saw a marked decline in the severity of warfare in Europe. The pitiless cruelty of the wars of religion seemed almost to have produced a revulsion. National states were already stabilizing but nationalism had not yet become a supreme ideal. The star of Hegel, whose philosophic basis for Prussian authoritarianism in the nineteenth century was to bear such baleful fruit in dictatorships of left and right in the twentieth was still below the horizon. There was nothing yet to take the place of the sectarian fanatic's impulse to destroy.

National ambitions were on the whole modest. They never went so far as to envisage the complete subjugation of a national adversary. A spirit of European community seemed to be developing. Rational speculation was increasing and with growing confidence in the future of man there was a tendency in human affairs to greater balance and restraint.

In a much-quoted passage Edward Gibbon, reviewing developments in the decades before 1770, wrote that Europe was becoming one great republic. 'The balance of power will fluctuate,' he said, 'but these partial events cannot essentially injure our general state of happiness.'[34] He was convinced that resort to fighting as a means of destroying the independence of other civilized peoples was at an end. The armed forces of Europe were now only exercised in 'temperate and undecisive conflicts'. The contenders, in fact, aimed at winning a modest purse on points, not a world title by a knockout.

Levels of technology were rising, and with them standards of living, but materials were still too scarce to sustain heavy fighting with improving techniques. War became a matter, in Defoe's words, of 'less blood and more money'.[35] Money was more than ever the key. 'Point d'argent, point de Suisses.'

Napoleon at Austerlitz (2 December 1805)

Following pages: The end of the Thirty Years War: the Treaty of Westphalia is successfully concluded, after eight years of negotiation, in Münster, 1648

75

1748. The French and the Allies join battle at Fontenoy in the War of the Austrian Succession, 1740–8 (Felix Philippoteaux, 1873)

Several factors in the make-up of eighteenth-century national standing armies helped to humanize war. Aristocratic officers found it difficult to hate men of the same sort as themselves merely because they were on the other side. National enthusiasms were rarely high. The quality of men in the ranks was generally low. Discipline was strict.

When decisive battles were fought they were often bloody. At the battle of Malplaquet (1709) in the Low Countries, forces fighting under Marlborough and Prince Eugene defeated the French under Villars in a 'deluge of blood', losing 22,000 men, or some 30 per cent[36] of their strength, as against 12,000 of the enemy. But decisive battles were rare. Marshal Saxe advised that battle should be avoided when possible because its outcome is uncertain and there are many advantages to be gained over the enemy without it. When it cannot be avoided, he advised, it must be won at all costs and where possible the enemy's retreat turned into utter rout.[37]

No longer did armies, as in the wars of religion, subsist almost entirely on the country. They now depended more on supply from magazines. This restricted their freedom of strategic and operational movement. At the same time the unreliability of the troops inhibited diffusion of command responsibility and reduced tactical flexibility.

Weapon techniques had improved but materials, including those required for shot and gunpowder, were scarce. For the saltpetre supplies essential to powder manufacture, animal sources were relied upon almost entirely. The saltpetre men pursued an active search for suitable nitrogenous substances in the stables, the birdhouses and even, in somewhat andalous fashion, the bedchambers of the citizen.[38] But even then there was still never enough powder to justify anything but careful use.

From the end of the period of military revolution, in the mid-seventeenth century, until the 1740s, France led the way in Western European military affairs. It is in France that the emergence of the standing army as an institution can best be studied and we have already been looking at it there. From the 1740s until the French Revolution the European military scene is dominated by Prussia. King Frederick William I of Prussia (1713–40) set up a conscript army under an iron code of discipline. His beheading of von Katte, the friend of his son Frederick, before the prince's own eyes, for trying to help the future Frederick the Great to escape from his father's tutelage, was typical of him. Von Katte had been condemned by the court to perpetual imprisonment. The king ordered otherwise.

In contemporary Western European armies severe punishments were not unknown – flogging, running the gauntlet, death by the hangman's halter or the firing squad – but the heavier penalties were rare and the administration of punishment generally rather haphazard. In the French army, indeed, flogging had never been customary. Under Frederick William I in Prussia discipline became vastly more severe.[39] The death penalty for minor infractions was not uncommon and flogging was regarded more or less as a matter of daily military administration. The dominant element in the management of soldiers was fear. Men went on into battle with at least a chance of survival. Withdrawal without orders was into certain death, as it is likely to be in the army of the U.S.S.R. today. Barrage battalions of the K.G.B., following up the advance, are there to see to that, as I am informed by a sometime officer of the Red Army. Frederick II, the Great, who succeeded his ferocious father in 1740, was a cultivated man, well educated and fond of music, tolerant in religious matters, once a friend of Voltaire and in some ways a typical product of the Enlightenment. But when he took on the military machine his father had developed he applied it in war with no relaxation of its brutal discipline.[40]

Casting cannon balls: the workman on the right is opening the mould (From Pyne, Microcosm, 1803–6)

Landsknechte are mustered and enrolled and their weapons examined (Contemporary engraving of 1621, Berlin)

Below: French Royal Magazine at the Bastille being shown off to foreign notables in the early eighteenth century (Le Pautre)

Right: French infantry drill according to the decree of 1766 (after Gravelot)

ARMES A PARIS
de la Bastille

'The life the private soldier led,' says Thackeray's Barry Lyndon, 'was a frightful one to any but men of iron courage and endurance.'[41] It was not then thought that satisfactory results could be secured by any other sort of treatment. The quality of the private soldier has rarely been lower than in the armies of mid-eighteenth-century Europe. In the contemporary European outlook there was no heroic view of war as an ennobling national experience. No especial esteem attached to a warrior class. The common soldier shared with the worker in some heavy industries, such as coal mining or iron founding, a position in society which was almost that of an outcast. No one enlisted unless he was nearly at the end of his tether.

The Comte de Guibert observed in a notable book written in 1772 that the profession of soldier had been abandoned 'to the most vile and miserable class of citizen'.[42] St Germain, as French Minister of War in 1775, was attracted by the Prussian system of conscript service, but rejected it because an army should 'consist of those for whom society has no use'.[43]

Recruiting into the armies of Europe in the mid-eighteenth century was often by force or fraud. To deaden the reluctance of all but the most wretched to endure the hardship of a private soldier's life, the two commonest anaesthetics of the age of the Enlightenment, the bottle and the club, were freely used.

The unwillingness of soldiery to be killed in a cause which did not greatly commend itself contributed to milder warfare, particularly when they were armed with better weapons. The bayonet, for example, which was originally developed for the protection of a hunter with an empty firearm against a wounded beast, perhaps originating in Bayonne, was issued to troops as a weapon of war in the 1680s.[44] It was at first plugged into the musket. Some time after 1690 the ring and socket was developed to enable the weapon to be fired with bayonet fixed. By the early eighteenth century the bayonet had virtually eliminated the difference between the pikeman and the musketeer.

It was in the armies of Frederick the Great that the bayonet was first generally found west of the Oder. But soldiers used it with little enthusiasm and were not easy to bring to close enough quarters for its application. Frightfulness is much more readily acceptable when it can be contrived at a distance. The bayonet helped to keep armies apart and thus contributed to those tendencies of the time which encouraged wars of position.

Desertion from the armies in the age of the Enlightenment was inevitably high. Frederick the Great gave his generals instructions at some length on how to prevent it by not, for example, camping too near woods, by avoiding night marches where possible, by patrols and guards around night dispositions less to keep the enemy out (the enemy had similar problems) than to keep his own men in, and so on.

'Our regiments,' says Frederick the Great in his *Instruction for His Generals*, 'are composed half of citizens and half of mercenaries. The latter, not attached to the state by any bonds of interest, become deserters at the first occasion.'[45]

'What cared I for their quarrels,' says Barry Lyndon, 'or whether the eagle under which I marched had one head or two?'[46]

Opposite: The future Frederick the Great obliged, as Crown Prince of Prussia, to witness from his prison cell the execution of his friend von Katte, under orders from his father King Frederick William I of Prussia, on 7 November 1730 (Copperplate engraving c.1740, Berlin)

A Grenadier of Frederick the Great's army (Lithograph of 1830, Berlin)

French infantry are dressed into line by a sergeant to fire a volley in the mid-eighteenth century

Even in the American revolutionary wars, at a time when the military calling was already rising somewhat in the esteem of the common man, the two sides were said to be largely composed of each other's deserters.[47]

In battle the eighteenth-century mercenary had even more compelling reasons to run away than usual. Thus evolutions in close order, inflexible and slow, carried out under the close supervision of the officers, were all that was possible. The armies of Frederick the Great were large single units moving into action with the general, whose business it was to lead them to the enemy and then set a good example. In the Seven Years War, fought between 1756 and 1763 largely as a result of Anglo-French colonial rivalries but involving Prussia, Austria and Russia as well, in an army whose total strength rarely exceeded 50,000 men, thirty-one Prussian generals were killed.

Officers in the eighteenth-century armies were not less exclusively aristocratic than they had been before armies stabilized into a regular pattern; they were more so. Officers from the bourgeoisie were not rare in the armies of Louis XIV. Frederick the Great combed them out of his. He was convinced that only aristocrats were sufficiently endowed with honour, courage and loyalty to make good officers and he was determined at the same time to bind the Junkers, the rising generation of reactionary Prussian nobility, to his own interests.

The aristocratic officer of the Enlightenment was usually brave and sometimes able, but he was rarely more than an amateur. Up to the eve of the Revolution in France promotion was by purchase, as it remained in England for another 100 years, although in both countries the highest military positions continued to be reserved to the highest nobility. The Comte du Guibert was the eighteenth-century author who perhaps came nearest to suggesting that warfare was an area of professional activity. His 'Essai Général de Tactique'[48] was almost prophetic in demanding a national citizen army and a war of movement. But he too insisted that command in war should be reserved to those whose birth and upbringing ensured that they possessed the necessary intuitive capacity. Even Henry Lloyd, the eighteenth-century Englishman whose approach to war was in some ways more sophisticated still, maintained that command in war was the product of natural genius. He divided warlike practice into two parts. The lower was mechanical and could be learned. The upper lay among the arts and excellence in it could be no more readily taught than in sculpture or music.[49]

The situation of Prussia under Frederick the Great brings a passing reminder of that of Sparta. Mirabeau said of it: '*La Prusse n'est pas un pays qui à une armée, c'est une armée qui à un pays.*'[50] The population of Prussia was only a small fraction of that of any of the neighbouring kingdom states – France, England, Austria, Russia. With hardly one-tenth of the population

Frederick the Great, in the Seven Years War, on the eve of his most skilfully conducted battle (in which he drove the Austrians from Silesia, at Leuthen on 5 December 1757) moves out with his Guards

of France, Prussia increased its army from 28,500 under Frederick William Hohenzollern the Great Elector (1640–88), to 83,000 in 1739, the last year of the reign of King Frederick William I. In that year Prussia still had less than 2 million inhabitants. Its industrial production was proportionately low. Nonetheless, Prussia was a major power in Western Europe. This was achieved in three ways: by subordinating almost all other considerations in the state to military strength; by setting a rational limit upon international ambitions; and by becoming the first state in Europe to make a serious business of war with explosives.

The military instrument of the Prussian experiment, the harshly disciplined and rigidly controlled force of unenthusiastic mercenaries, became the model for the armies of Europe, armies in which, as the Great Frederick himself said, 'obedience . . . is so exact that . . . however little a general knows how to make himself obeyed, he is bound to be'.[51]

The European system of standing armies was destroyed by the French Revolution. The removal of barriers within the nation, the rejection of caste exclusiveness in national administration, the disappearance of the deadweight of absolutist forms of government too rigid to be easily modified, all helped to release in France a flood of national feeling. Freedom was everywhere, in the negative but nonetheless real sense of the removal of restraints. Like any other career a military career was now to be open to the talents. The elective principle was introduced for the promotion of N.C.O.s and officers, in spite of its recent failure in the American revolutionary armies. Recruiting at first remained voluntary.[52]

Under the growing threat of invasion, however, conscription was introduced into the French army in the *levée en masse* of 1793. The elective principle of promotion was soon forgotten. It was true that careers remained open to the talents, but military talents were predominantly disclosed where they might have been expected to occur, that is, among the officers and men already serving under arms at the time of the Revolution. Six of Napoleon's twenty-five future marshals of France (I have not counted Poniatowski who was not a Frenchman but a Pole and was only a marshal for a very short while anyway) were at this time civilians but the other nineteen were already serving. Nine of them were already officers and every one of these was noble (though mostly of the lower orders) while only ten of the twenty-five were common soldiers.

What was new in a Europe in which war had recently been little more than the sport of kings was the enthusiasm of a revolutionary nation in arms. In this the impulse to defend the Revolution was fused with and then dominated by a passion to defend the country, just as in Soviet Russia in the Second World War.

The nature of the French armies which were now being raised largely dictated their operating methods. Masses of ill-trained men could not hope to operate in the closely disciplined linear formations of Frederician mercenaries. The inclination of French revolutionary troops was to attack. This they did in mobs dignified by the name of 'columns' but mobs nonetheless, surrounded by skirmishing infantry, the *tirailleurs*.

The regulated musketry of the Prussian platoons, with volley fire and evolutions like the countermarch, were quite beyond them. Instead, the *tirailleurs* acted as individual marksmen, moving with great freedom and making good use of cover. Their adversaries, using cover scarcely at all, stood, fired and fell in close order. The general direction of advance of the large irregular groups in which the main body of the French infantry was assembled could be more readily controlled than if they were dressed in horizontal lines. When the French columns charged with the bayonet they carried with them something of the blood lust of a revolutionary mob. Their aim was the total destruction of the enemy; humanitarian scruples were few. The age of limited war was over.

It is sad that we have so little original source material, before the nineteenth century, coming from fighting men who were not officers, or of the officer class. The reasons are obvious enough. The Recollections of Rifleman Harris, *edited by one Captain Curling and published in 1848, are among the earliest we have and are of quite outstanding interest. How far they were polished in the editorial process it is hard to say, but a high degree of authenticity is generally conceded to the published text.*

Napoleon, prevented from destroying Britain by its navy, concentrated after Trafalgar (1805) on the development of his 'Continental System', which was in the event to prove his undoing. This led him quite early on to interference in Portugal, Britain's 'oldest European ally' and readily accessible by sea. Britain landed troops, to come under command of Arthur Wellesley, the man who later as the Duke of Wellington was to crush Napoleon at Waterloo.

Rifleman Harris served in the 95th Regiment of Foot, later to be known under the famous name of the Rifle Brigade. He describes here the successful action fought against the French at Vimiero (spelled in British battle honours Vimiera) *very soon after the troops landed, when the 95th was in Fane's brigade. We are shown a vignette of the new way of war that was beginning to sweep through the Western world, as seen by an infantry soldier fighting in the ranks. I know of few better accounts of an infantry engagement.*

It was on the 21st of August that we commenced fighting the battle of Vimiero.

The French came down upon us in a column, and the Riflemen immediately commenced a sharp fire upon them from whatever cover they could get a shelter behind, whilst our cannon played upon them from our rear. I saw regular lanes torn through their ranks as they advanced, which were immediately closed up again as they marched steadily on. Whenever we saw a round shot thus go through the mass we raised a shout of delight.

One of our corporals, named Murphy, was the first man in the Rifles who was hit that morning, and I remember more particularly remarking the circumstance from his apparently having a presentiment of his fate before the battle began. He was usually an active fellow, and up to this time had shown himself a good and brave soldier, but on this morning he seemed unequal to his duty. General [Henry] Fane and Major [Robert] Travers were standing together on an early part of this day. The general had a spy-glass in his hand, and for some time looked anxiously at the enemy. Suddenly he gave the word to fall in, and immediately all was bustle amongst us. The Honourable Captain Pakenham spoke very sharply to Murphy, who appeared quite dejected and out of spirits, I observed. He had a presentiment of death, which is by no means an uncommon circumstance, and I have observed it once or twice since this battle.

Others beside myself noticed Murphy on this morning, and as we had reason to know he was not ordinarily deficient in courage, the circumstance was talked of after the battle was over. He was the first man shot that day.

Just before the battle commenced in earnest, and whilst the officers were busily engaged with their companies, shouting the word of command, and arranging matters of moment, Captain Leech ordered a section of our men to move off, at double quick, and take possession of a windmill, which was on our left. I was amongst this section, and set off full cry towards the mill, when Captain Leech espied and roared out to me by name to return – 'Hello there! you Harris!' he called, 'fall out of that section directly. We want you here, my man.' I, therefore, wheeled out of the rank, and returned to him. 'You fall in amongst the men here, Harris,' he said, 'I shall not send you to that post. The cannon will play upon the mill in a few moments like hail; and what shall we do,' he continued laughing, 'without our head shoemaker to repair our shoes?' . . .

The first cannon shot I saw fired, I remember, was a miss. The artilleryman made a sad bungle, and the ball went wide of the mark. We were all looking anxiously to see the effect of this shot; and another of the gunners (a red-haired man) rushed at the fellow who had fired, and in the excitement of the moment, knocked him head over heels with his fists. 'D— you for a fool,' he said; 'what sort of a shot do you call that? Let me take the gun.' He accordingly fired the next shot himself, as soon as the gun was loaded, and so truly did he point it at the French column on the hillside, that we saw the fatal effect of the destructive missile by the lane it made and the confusion it caused.

Our Riflemen (who at the moment were amongst the guns) upon seeing this, set up a tremendous shout of delight, and the battle commencing immediately, we were all soon hard at work.

I myself was very soon so hotly engaged, loading and firing away, enveloped in the smoke I created, and the cloud which hung about me from the continued fire of my comrades, that I could see nothing for a few minutes but the red flash of my own piece amongst the white vapour clinging to my very clothes. This has often seemed to me the greatest drawback upon our present system of fighting; for whilst in such state, on a calm day, until some friendly breeze of wind clears the space around, a soldier knows no more of his position and what is about to happen in his front, or what has happened (even amongst his own companions) than the very dead lying around.

Such is my remembrance of the commencement of the battle of Vimiero. The battle began on a fine bright day, and the sun played on the arms of the enemy's battalions, as they came on, as if they had been tipped with gold. The battle soon became general; the smoke thickened around, and often I was obliged to stop firing and dash it aside from my face, and try in vain to get sight of what was going on, whilst groans and shouts and a noise of cannon and musketry appeared almost to shake the very ground. It seemed hell upon earth, I thought.

. . . During the battle I remarked the gallant style in which the 50th, Major [Charles] Napier's regiment, came to the charge. They dashed upon the enemy like a torrent breaking bounds and the French, unable even to bear the sight of them, turned and fled. Methinks at this moment I can hear the cheers of the British soldiers in the charge, and the clatter of the Frenchmen's accoutrements, as they turned in an instant, and went off as hard as they could run for it. I remember, too, our feelings towards the enemy on that occasion was the north side of friendly, for they had been firing upon us Rifles very sharply, greatly outnumbering our skirmishers, and appearing inclined to drive us off the face of the earth. Their Lights, and Grenadiers, I, for the first time, particularly remarked on that day. The Grenadiers (the 70th, I think), our men seemed to know well. They were all fine-looking young men, wearing red shoulder-knots and tremendous-looking moustaches. As they came swarming upon us, they rained a perfect shower of balls, which we returned quite as sharply. Whenever one of them was knocked over our men called out, 'There goes another of Boney's Invincibles.'

In the main body immediately in our rear, were the second battalion 52nd, the 50th, the second battalion 43rd, and a German corps, whose number I do not remember, besides several other regiments. The whole line seemed annoyed and angered at seeing the Rifles outnumbered by the Invincibles, and as we fell back 'firing and retiring', galling them handsomely as we did so, the men cried out (as it were with one voice) to charge. 'D—n them!' they roared, 'charge! charge!' General Fane, however, restrained their impetuosity. He desired them to stand fast and keep their ground.

'Don't be too eager, men,' he said, as coolly as if we were on drill-parade in old England; 'I don't want you to advance just yet. Well done, 95th!' he called out, as he galloped up and down the line; 'well done, 43rd, 52nd, and well done all. I'll not forget, if I live, to report your conduct to-day. They shall hear of it in England, my lads!'

A man named Brotherwood, of the 95th, at this moment rushed up to the general, and presented him with a green feather, which he had torn out of the cap of a French light-infantry soldier he had killed. 'God bless you, general!' he said; 'wear this for the sake of the 95th.' I saw the general take the feather and stick it in his cocked hat. The next minute he gave the word to charge, and down came the whole line, through a tremendous fire of cannon and musketry – and dreadful

'The Organizer of
Victory': Napoleon
thus designated
Lazare-Nicolas-Marguerite
Canot (1753–1823),
War Minister of France
1793–5

was the slaughter as they rushed onwards. As they came up with us, we sprang to our feet, gave one hearty cheer, and charged along with them, treading over our own dead and wounded, who lay in the front. The 50th were next us as we went, and I recollect, as I said, the firmness of that regiment in the charge. They appeared like a wall of iron. The enemy turned and fled, the cavalry dashing upon them as they went off.

Note: *In the British army's regimental system the 50th Foot is today a component in the Queen's Regiment. The 43rd and 52nd together form the First Royal Green Jackets. The Rifle Brigade, the old 95th, is now the Third Royal Green Jackets. The Second R.G.J., as a matter of interest, is the former King's Royal Rifle Corps, one of whose earliest titles was 'The Loyal Americans'. In an army in which the regimental system, with all its (perhaps sometimes avoidable) inconveniences, is a major source of strength, there are few examples of more tenacious loyalties, more idiosyncratic behaviour and more distinguished performance on the battlefield than those shown by these rifle regiments.*

Working beside social processes towards the evolution of new forms of war were technical ones. The mobilization of the whole manpower of a nation would not have been possible without the great expansion in industrial production which took place in the late eighteenth century. A marked increase in the output of metals was one notable consequence of this. Increased use of artillery resulted. Accuracy and rapidity of fire were the result of improved methods, as France took the lead in applying mathematics to military purposes. Monge, Minister of Marine, was said to be the inventor of descriptive geometry. Carnot, Minister of War, whom Napoleon described as the architect of victory, was another distinguished mathematician.[53] Reduction in weight of artillery pieces resulted from better design. This in turn led to higher mobility. Better road surfaces made movement easier. A return to the practice of living off the country cut down impedimenta and reduced the dependence of field forces on supply depots.

The technical prerequisites for the operations of mass armies in war already existed by the close of the eighteenth century. The revolutionary government was able to exploit them. A national army, raised under a universal obligation to serve, harmonized with the new society. Higher cohesion within the army permitted a greater spread of command responsibility in the field. Desertion, though not uncommon in Napoleon's later years (it was particularly noticeable in the Russian campaign of 1812), never exercised a formative influence on tactics as it did with Frederick the Great.

In the French revolutionary armies a new looseness and freedom now developed, with a predominantly offensive spirit. The combination of increases in mass, flexibility, offensive outlook and fire power resulted in a revolution in tactics.

Better gunnery methods soon led to more effective results. The practice developed by Napoleon, himself a gunner, was to direct concentrated

Following pages:
Austerlitz, 2 December
1805: the Emperor
Napoleon outmanoeuvres
and routs the armies of
Austria and Russia. The
casualties on both sides
amounted to an estimated
25,000

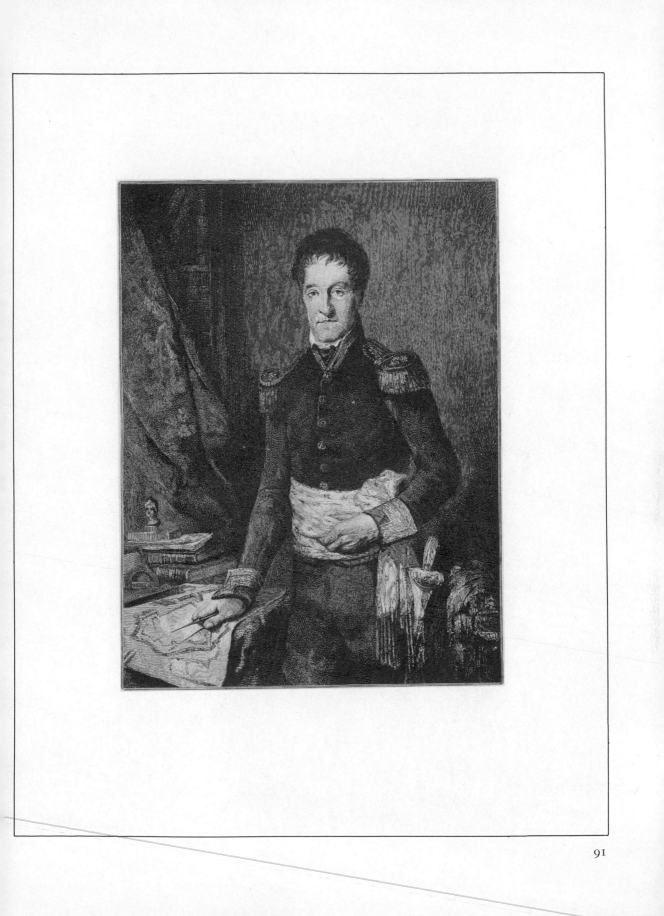

Monument to the Revolution commemorating Valmy at Méry (Aube, 25 km. south-east of Paris)

Opposite: Napoleon's retreat from Moscow, 1812: a wounded Guardsman leads a blinded Cuirassier through the snow

The French repulse the Prussians at Valmy, 20 September 1792: this was the opening, in Goethe's words, of 'a new epoch in world history'

artillery fire against a chosen infantry target until it began to weaken and then to assault at its weakest point with the bayonets of his own infantry. Plentiful munitions and higher mobility made it possible to repeat the process. Cavalry kept for shock action at speed could now turn defeat into disaster and retreat into rout. Thus it was, for example, that a French army 65,000 strong destroyed an army of 83,000 Russians and Austrians at Austerlitz in 1805. This was the method used in most of Napoleon's classic victories, a method admirably suited to Napoleon's opportunist approach, impossible to apply a hundred years before but still the basis of battlefield tactics a hundred years later.

The development of an enthusiasm for military exploits in the masses, almost unknown in the previous century, together with material progress of many kinds and increased administrative skills, made it possible in the early nineteenth century to keep in the field armies of four or five times the size of those maintained in the religious wars two centuries before. Casualties also rose. When the Duke of Brunswick's well-drilled Prussians were routed on 20 September 1792 by the citizen battalions of Champagne at Valmy, a battle had been fought which was of critical importance. Goethe, who was present, said to his companions: 'From here and from today begins a new epoch in world history, and you can say that you were there when it opened.'[54] But at Valmy no more than a few hundred men were killed. At Austerlitz thirteen years later the casualties numbered 25,000. The Moscow campaign of 1812 cost France in dead, wounded, prisoners, missing and deserters, half a million men. All other considerations apart, exhaustion of manpower and to a considerable extent exhaustion of materials (particularly metals) helped to ensure that peace would follow the final disappearance of Napoleon.

Conscripts for Napoleon's armies. A drawing said to have been made from an actual occurrence in January 1807

The Nineteenth Century Officer

The eighteenth century had seen the regularization of armed service in Western Europe. In the nineteenth true professionalism emerges. Before 1800 there was virtually no such thing as a professional officer corps anywhere. After 1900 no sovereign power of any significance, either in the old world or the new, was without one. The timing and manner of this development was different in different countries. It happened earliest and most completely in Germany.

A current of opinion already flowing in Prussia during the last years of the old century became a torrent in the early years of the new. It burst its banks in 1806 after Jena. Prussia's problem was to find a defence against the almost irresistible national armies of Napoleon. To many officers it seemed that the only way of doing this was to tap the same sort of resources. Gneisenau pleaded that the Germans should mobilize the whole strength of the people as the French had done. The old rigid formulae bequeathed by Frederick the Great, governing the use of relatively small formations of heavily disciplined mercenaries, were not enough. 'Get us a national army,' said Blücher, urging that the Prussians forget their 'useless pedantries'.[55]

General conscription was not easily introduced in Prussia. Not until March 1813, when Prussia in alliance with Russia declared war on France, did the *Landwehr* edict set up an embodied militia. Only in September 1814 was military service made obligatory, without exemption, on every able-bodied male. The system which was then introduced of five years' service in the regular army followed by fourteen in the *Landwehr* remained in force with little change until the First World War.

Meanwhile the restrictions which confined entry into the Prussian officer corps almost exclusively to aristocrats had been modified. A decree of the Prussian government of 6 August 1808 bluntly declared: 'All previously existing class preference in the military establishment is abolished, and every man, without regard to his origins, has equal duties and equal rights.'[56]

King Frederick William III of Prussia, freed by the disastrous campaign of 1812 from his subservience to France, joins Czar Alexander I of Russia in opposition to Napoleon, 17 March 1813 (By Georg Bleibtreu, reproduced in Deutsche Gedenkhalle)

The principle thus enunciated was only imperfectly observed, even in Prussia, and to a varying degree at different periods in different countries. But its explicit formulation marked an abrupt end to the hitherto scarcely questioned assumption that only by noble birth was a man entitled to claim military command, or endowed with the intuitive capacity to exercise it. At the same time innovations were made in operational practice. Linear tactics, platoon fire, close formations began to be replaced by the dispersed approach and individual marksmanship of the French.

Neither the inroads on the aristocratic monopoly of the officer's career nor these tactical innovations found much favour with the Prussian old guard. *Tirailleur* tactics were 'suspicious in political respects and superfluous in military'. Dispersed fighting might be good enough for the French – 'a vivacious race' – but it was entirely unsuited to the Prussian. It was dishonouring, in fact, to the national character to substitute organized disorder for the famous Prussian platoon musketry.[57]

Franco-Prussian War, 1870–1: idealized and not wholly credible picture of the Prussian Guard advancing at Sedan, 1 September 1870, when the French Army under Maréchal MacMahon was forced to capitulate

There was an unusual feature of the reforms of Scharnhorst, Gneisenau, Blücher, Grolman and the Prussian Military Commission, reforms which were the real basis of the growth of military professionalism in the Western world. Modifications in civil institutions are often the cause of military reforms. It is rare to find civil reforms springing from a requirement to modify military practice. This, however, is what happened to Prussia.

The national enthusiasm which alone could enable a German mass army to defeat the French was unlikely to develop among serfs. Emancipation was inevitable. At the same time agrarian reform, some rationalizing of taxation, a lightening of vestigial feudal burdens on trade and other acts of recognition of the importance of the individual seem to have done much to encourage support throughout Germany, both of peasants and bourgeoisie, for the effort to withstand the Napoleonic armies in the field. These social reforms were radical but not revolutionary. It is very doubtful if they would have occurred when they did without the pressure of a military requirement. They were hardly the precursors of permanent and irreversible change. Indeed, the monarch who had presided over their introduction, King Frederick William III, when the military threat to Prussia had receded, was himself largely responsible for a period of reaction which did much to negate them.

The completeness of the change from the military system of Frederick the Great to that under which the War of Liberation was fought is suggested by changes in command. Of the 143 Prussian general officers on active duty in 1803 only eight remained in 1812. Of these only two (one of them Blücher) held commands at the time of Napoleon's overthrow.[58]

A thoroughgoing revision of the composition and preparation of the officer establishment was as important as the creation of a mass army. The victory which Germany was to win over France in 1870 was not simply the victory of what had by then become a nation in arms over what had then become a professional army. It was the victory of a nation which had taken professionalism in the profession of arms more seriously.

It was also the victory of a nation, the Prussian, which in quite a short space of time had been deliberately refashioned in an absolutist pattern.

It is probably as difficult to cause a nation to change course along lines essentially alien to its nature as it is to induce a fundamentally uncharacteristic action from a patient under hypnosis. There may be a parallel here. It has been said of the sad and often sullen resignation of late twentieth-century Russians to the total supremacy of the Communist Party of the Soviet Union that, since the Russians had been slaves under the Tartars and serfs under the Tsars, they were ripely conditioned for servitude under the Commissars. The suggestion here is that nations tend to follow their own bent. Unfriendly critics of the English, for example, may argue that centuries of piracy and generations of imperial predation have produced a bottled-up head of aggressive energy which now finds its chief outlet in hooliganism at international football fixtures. I do not pursue this further, except to suggest that different nations have quite different characteristics and to add that these are not always sufficiently understood, whether by foreigners or nationals, least of all, perhaps, by the latter.

The philosophic basis of twentieth-century totalitarianism is largely found in the teachings of Georg Wilhelm Friedrich Hegel, philosopher-in-chief to King Frederick William III of Prussia, whose reaction to liberal values was intense

The most promising country for the launching of revolutionary socialism, in the eyes of Karl Marx, was industrial Britain. In all the century and a quarter since the publication of *Das Kapital*, it has never, in fact, really got off the ground. The country where it eventually flourished was perhaps the least promising of all – archaic, agricultural, feudal Russia. Nations can be pushed along, but never, it would seem, in directions wholly repugnant to them. Fascists were not lacking, between the two world wars of this century, in any major country. It was only in three, Spain, Italy and Germany, that they were made sufficiently welcome to be able to take over. A nation can be moulded and guided but the mould into which it eventually moves must be one to which it is fundamentally inclined.

My purpose here is to examine the profession of arms, not the position of professors of philosophy, but it would be wrong to take no notice of one of them. This is Hegel, whose influence ('and especially,' says Karl Popper, 'that of his cant') is still very powerful, as Popper has pointed out, on the Marxist extreme left and the neo-Fascist extreme right.

When in 1815, with the French grip loosed, reactionary politics began once again to dominate Prussia, King Frederick William III, having shed the liberalizing and reforming political influences which had been so useful in the War of Liberation with France, was in need of an ideology. Hegel was brought to Berlin in 1818 to furnish it and, until his death in 1831, applied a powerful mind to the justification of a total state absolutism in the person of the monarch. Hegel represents the pure philosophic essence of modern totalitarianism. The national outlook developed in Prussia by the absolute monarch whose lackey (in Schopenauer's term) Hegel became, was to be reflected in the pattern, public position and general outlook of the Prussian army for nearly another century.

The rigid pattern of the military system of Frederick the Great had dissolved during the Napoleonic struggles and would never be reconstituted.

Class barriers on officer entry had now been lowered. What was wanted next was a liberally educated body of officers ('*ein gebildetes Offizierkorps*'), then a professionally educated body of officers ('*ein berufsgebildetes Offizierkorps*') and finally a structure of promotion in which criteria of competence should predominate. The integration of the profession into the society it had grown up to serve was to remain a problem. After the total defeat of Germany in two world wars, whose aftermath in each case saw radical change in the relationship between civil and military, it still does.

In Prussia under the reforms of 1806–12 officer-candidates had to graduate from the gymnasia with a certificate of fitness to enter a university, or pass a rigorous six-day general examination designed to test mental capacity rather than factual knowledge. Scharnhorst introduced examinations as a condition for promotion. He also raised officers' pay to reduce reliance on outside resources. More important still, perhaps, he established in 1810 the Kriegsakademie in Berlin, which was for a long time the only institution in Europe for the advanced study of war and the higher education of officers in non-warlike disciplines. Forty officers were selected annually by rigorous examination after a minimum of five years' service.

Russian agriculture, in an ancient, long-persistent mode, savagely attacked under the Marxist-Leninist régime

Attendance at the academy became before long almost a condition of high advancement. The effect of what was in fact already a well-developed military educational system is suggested by an estimate that in 1859 about 50 per cent of the military literature in Europe was produced in Germany. Twenty-five per cent in that year came from France. One per cent came from England.[59]

In France, though several specialist military schools grew up in the early nineteenth century, the only one attempting to do anything similar was the staff school (Ecole d'Etat Major) set up by St Cyr in 1818, the year, it so happens, which saw Hegel's removal to Berlin, at King Frederick William III's wish, to become the supreme ideologist of Prussian absolutism. The French military attaché in Berlin was moved to observe in 1860 that all French military educational institutions were only agricultural schools by comparison with the Kriegsakademie. It was not till after the disaster of 1870 that the French made a real effort to develop the education of their officers.

The foundation of the Ecole Militaire Supérieure in 1878 was to open a new chapter.

As France continued to lag behind Germany, England, though the beginnings of true professionalism had manifested themselves in her navy, was in her army further behind still. A school opened in 1799 by the Duke of York to educate officers for the staff was reorganized in 1802 as the Royal Military College, with a staff course as its senior department.[60] Only in 1857, however, when the senior department was detached as the nucleus of the Staff College, did Britain begin to make any real progress in professional military education. Progress was not fast. An English observer noted in 1859 that the devotion of the Prussian officer to education, no less than the certainty of promotion through merit and not from caprice, set Prussian officers on the whole far above those found in the English army.[61]

That part of the English public school output which went into the army was not notable for its academic attainment. What was wanted was the sort of young man, according to the Duke of Wellington, who could go straight from school with two N.C.O.s and fifteen private soldiers and get a shipload of convicts to Australia without trouble.[62]

So long as purchase existed in the British army a true system of professional advancement was impossible. By 1856 a captaincy cost some £2,400, a lieutenant-colonelcy £7,000. Officers' pay stood at the same level as 150 years before. The Duke of Wellington was not in favour of reform and those who thought with him resisted it. They opposed the substitution of what they called a mercenary army for one whose officers were men of substance, with a real interest in the preservation of the existing social order. Only the demonstration of Prussian military efficiency offered by the French *débâcle* of 1870 enabled Edward Cardwell to abolish purchase in 1871.[63] But as late as 1890 it was possible for a British general to say that England was still split between those who adhered to the tradition of Wellington and those who wished to make the army a profession.[64]

continued on page 121

*Above: Rocroi, 18 May 1643:
Louis de Bourbon (1621-86),
Duc d'Enghien, defeats Don
Francisco del Melo and breaks
the power of the old Spanish
'tercio', the latter-day legion.
This was a disastrous blow to
Spain (Chantilly, Musée
Condé)*

*French soldiers of the sixteenth
century (from a lithograph by
Charpentier: Firmin Didot)*

Left: Two scenes showing French soldiers and officers of the seventeenth century (from a lithograph by Lestel: Firmin Didot, Paris)

Below left: German soldiers of the seventeenth century, the period of the Thirty Years War, one of whose foremost figures was Wallenstein, seen in the bottom picture wearing a yellow coat. Wallenstein served the Catholic Emperor against the Protestants of the north, in a brilliant career which brought him wealth and fame but whose devious path led to his murder. He is likely to be long remembered for his fervent dreams of German unity (From a lithograph published by Fr. E. Kohler)

Below: French uniforms and costumes of 1750 (from a lithograph published by Fr. E. Kohler)

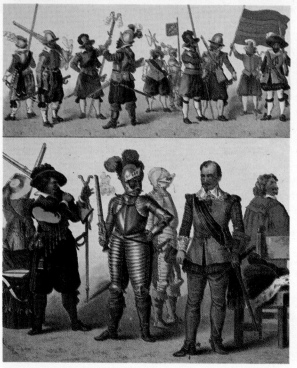

Above: 1688 – the raising at Reading in England of the regiment of Colonel Archibald Douglas. This became the 16th Foot and later the Bedfordshire and Hertfordshire Regiment, and is now absorbed into the Royal Anglian Regiment. The initial cadre of officers and N.C.O.s came from the Royal Scots, veterans of Tangier and Sedgemoor (C.C.P. Lawson, 1938, National Army Museum, London)

Officers and Gentlemen of the French Maison du Roi 1675 (Musée des Arts Decoratifs, Paris)

Claude-Victor (1764–1841), Duke of Belluno (or Bellune) and Marshal of the Empire, began his military career under the Old Régime as a drummer, and attracted Napoleon's attention at the siege of Toulon, 1793. After much success he was soundly defeated by Sir Thomas Graham at Barrosa in Spain, 5 March 1811 (Picture by Antoine-Jean-Gros)

Print of a private of the Royal North British Fusiliers, 1742

British redcoats march into battle in the Seven Years' War: a still from the film Barry Lyndon, *made from Thackeray's novel*

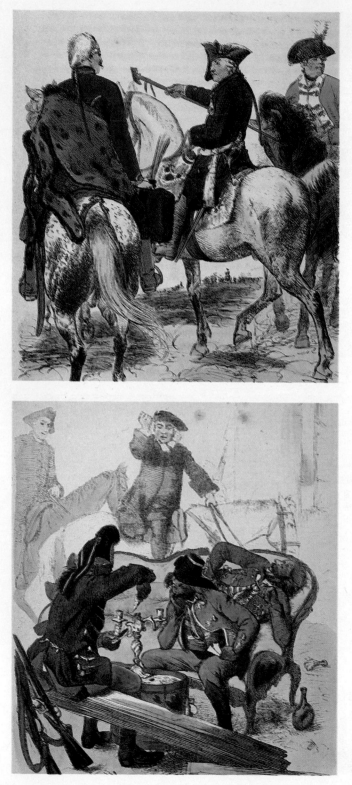

King Frederick II of Prussia, Frederick the Great (By A. Menzel)

Grenadiers of Napoleon's Old Guard in campaign of France moving in column platoons through Champagne in 1814. the background the Emperor uses a spy-gl steadied on a Hussar's shoulder. In foreground lies a dead Prussian off. (By A. Bligh

Retreat from Moscow 1812. The 2. Chasseurs à Cheval, commanded Colonel Marcelin de Marbot, foraging beef in Byelorussia (By Myrbec

Army chaplain confronts looters from a Prussian Freikorps in the Seven Years' War (By A. Menzel)

Left: Lieutenant Dieudonné of the Chasseurs à Cheval, Old Guard, leading a charge. This picture by Géricault was shown in the Salon of 1812, the year in which its subject was killed near Vilna

Right: Bonaparte explaining his plan for the taking of Toulon in 1793 (From a painting by André Castaigne)

Above: Royal Regiment of
Artillery in France in the
time of Louis XV. Taken
from Moltzheim,
L'Artillerie française
(Musée de l'Armée, Paris)

Left: French siege artillery
in 1775, in the time of Louis
XVI (Musée de l'Armée,
Paris)

Above right: Austerlitz,
2 December 1805.
Napoleon defeats the
Austrian and Russian
imperial armies in the
'Battle of Three Emperors'

Right: The Imperial French
Army, under Napoleon,
enters Moscow,
14 September 1812

Above: Murat leading the cavalry in the defeat of the Prussians at Jena, 14 October 1806 (From the painting by H. Chartier, 1895)

The Prussians under Blücher checked by Napoleon at Ligny, 16 June 1815, in their attempt to join up with Wellington. Gneisenau is here giving orders for the withdrawal to Wavre (Picture by Richard Knote)

The Duke of Wellington visiting outposts at Soignies, June 1815 (Picture by Hippolyte Lecomte, 1781–1857, Apsley House)

Below: 'Custer's last stand'. Action of the 7th United States Cavalry under General George Armstrong Custer at the Little Big Horn on 25 June 1876: one of the best known episodes in the Indian Wars (Picture by Otto Becker)

French colonial soldiers of the 1880s armed with the Lebel rifle whose tubular magazine would soon give way to the box magazine

Below: 'The Last Cartridges', a picture by Alphonse de Neuville of an incident in the Franco-Prussian War at Bazeilles on 31 August 1870, in a battle of the Sedan campaign in which Maréchal MacMahon was wounded. The Chassepot rifle seen here, an advanced form of single-shot breech-loader with a paper cartridge (soon to be replaced by a brass cartridge), was greatly superior to the German needle-gun

Above: 29th Bombay Native Infantry in the British Service, armed with the Snider single-shot breech-loading rifle, the first Service rifle with a metallic cartridge case

British troops in action against Boers during the Siege of Mafeking in the South African War 1899 (By R. Caton Woodville)

Above: British Royal Horse Artillery in South Africa, 1900 (By George Scott: National Army Museum, London)

British wars in Zululand. Isandhlwana, 22 January 1879. Lieutenants Melville (in red patrol jacket) and Coghill defending the Queen's colour of the 1/24th. Both were posthumously awarded the Victoria Cross (By A. de Neuville, 1835–85, National Army Museum, London)

continued from page 104

Wellington's organization and use of his army has been described as marking in many ways the high watermark of eighteenth-century warfare. He had no great regard for soldiers. He was determined to defend his country and at the same time a social system of which an officer class drawn exclusively from its upper levels and a body of soldiery drawn almost entirely from its lowest were characteristic. Sir John Fortescue said of him that 'he believed in the England that produced such gentlemen and was resolved to save her and them. He took over his army as an instrument to that end . . . but, when his purpose was fulfilled, he threw the instrument aside without compunction, having no further use for it and little or no sentiment about it.'[65]

England, busy with her industrial development, was safe behind a sea barrier at home while abroad she pursued a policy of colonial expansion and of foreign trade based on naval supremacy. The value of a navy to her material interests was much more readily apparent than any an army could offer. In consequence, though the professional standing of naval officers was developing, she was very slow to recognize the need for professionalism in the officers of her army. For almost exactly 100 years after Waterloo, England did not have to meet anything approaching an equal on the battlefield, with the exception of the grossly mismanaged war in the Crimea against the Russians, in alliance with French and Turks, in 1854. Her wars were otherwise the wars of expanding empire. Her army officers were gentlemen first, landed gentry almost always, professionals almost never. Her common soldiers were the restless, the misfits, the unhappy. For most of the nineteenth century they achieved little more than the standing of second-class citizens.[66]

Winston Churchill, twenty-four years of age, and a regular officer in the 4th Queen's Own Hussars but cherishing ambitions in journalism and politics, was serving in India in 1898, as the campaign for the British repossession of the Sudan (evacuated under pressure from the Mahdi in 1895) gathered way. He had secured a lucrative contract to report what his own book later described as 'The River War' for the London Morning Post, *and wanted to be where the action was. The 21st Lancers of the British Army were serving in the Sudan at the time, in what was in fact an Egyptian army under Kitchener as 'Sirdar'. Kitchener would not have the young Churchill at any price. Influence generated by his late father, Lord Randolph Churchill, a former Cabinet Minister of high distinction, wielded by his American mother, was sufficient to get him attached to the 21st Lancers nonetheless. He was thus able to take part in that regiment's charge at the Battle of Omdurman, a battle in which the army of the Khalifa, the Mahdi's successor, fighting most bravely against a smaller force with greatly superior weapon power, was destroyed losing 11,000 men killed. This led in the event to the restoration of British sovereignty over Egypt and the Sudan.*

Winston Churchill, after a remarkably courageous spell as a war correspondent in the Boer War that followed in South Africa, left soldiering for politics in 1900. Half a century later he was to become, under the British Army's regimental system, Colonel of the 4th Queen's Own Hussars and thereafter of the Queen's Royal Irish

A recruiting party in 1813 for the 33rd Regiment (of which Wellington was once Colonel)

Hussars, when the 4th Hussars were amalgamated with the 8th King's Royal Irish Hussars to form that regiment. He remained the regimental Colonel until his death. A few years later I took over the same Colonelcy.

Winston Churchill's attachment to the 4th Hussars never weakened. He was determined, he said, to have Hussars at his funeral. To the 21st Lancers he never paid much attention.

Here is his account of the charge of the 21st Lancers at Omdurman.

Everyone expected that we were going to make a charge. That was the one idea that had been in all minds since we had started from Cairo. Of course there would be a charge. In those days, before the Boer War, British cavalry had been taught little else. Here was clearly the occasion for a charge. But against what body of enemy, over what ground, in which direction or with what purpose, were matters hidden from the rank and file. We continued to pace forward over the hard sand, peering into the mirage-twisted plain in a high state of suppressed excitement. Presently I noticed 300 yards away on our flank and parallel to the line on which we were advancing, a long row of blue-black objects, two or three yards apart. I thought there were about a hundred and fifty. Then I became sure that these were men — enemy men — squatting on the ground. Almost at the same moment the trumpet sounded 'Trot', and the whole long column of cavalry began to jingle and clatter across the front of these crouching figures. We were in the lull of the battle and there was perfect silence. Forthwith from every blue-black blob came a white puff of smoke, and a loud volley of musketry broke the odd stillness. Such a target at such a distance could scarcely be missed, and all along the column here and there horses bounded and a few men fell.

Opposite: British recruiting sergeant, 1815

123

The intentions of our Colonel had no doubt been to move round the flank of the body of Dervishes he had now located, and who, concealed in a fold of the ground behind their riflemen, were invisible to us, and then to attack them from a more advantageous quarter; but once the fire was opened and losses began to grow, he must have judged it inexpedient to prolong his procession across the open plain. The trumpet sounded 'Right wheel into line', and all the sixteen troops swung round towards the blue-black riflemen. Almost immediately the regiment broke into a gallop, and the 21st Lancers were committed to their first charge in war!

I propose to describe exactly what happened to me: what I saw and what I felt. I recalled it to my mind so frequently after the event that the impression is as clear and vivid as it was a quarter of a century ago. The troop I commanded was, when we wheeled into line, the second from the right of the regiment. I was riding a handy, sure-footed grey Arab polo pony. Before we wheeled and began to gallop, the officers had been marching with drawn swords. On account of my shoulder I had always decided that if I were involved in hand-to-hand fighting, I must use a pistol and not a sword. I had purchased in London a Mauser automatic pistol, then the newest and the latest design. I had practised carefully with this during our march and journey up the river. This then was the weapon with which I determined to fight. I had first of all to return my sword into its scabbard, which is not the easiest thing to do at a gallop. I had then to draw my pistol from its wooden holster and bring it to full cock. This dual operation took an appreciable time, and until it was finished, apart from a few glances to my left to see what effect the fire was producing, I did not look up at the general scene.

Then I saw immediately before me, and now only half the length of a polo ground away, the row of crouching blue figures firing frantically, wreathed in white smoke. On my right and left my neighbouring troops leaders made a good line. Immediately behind was a long dancing row of lances couched for the charge. We were going at a fast but steady gallop. There was too much trampling and rifle fire to hear any bullets. After this glance to the right and left and at my troop, I looked again towards the enemy. The scene appeared to be suddenly transformed. The blue-black men were still firing, but behind them there now came into view a depression like a shallow sunken road. This was crowded and crammed with men rising up from the ground where they had hidden. Bright flags appeared as if by magic, and I saw arriving from nowhere Emirs on horseback among and around the mass of the enemy. The Dervishes appeared to be ten or twelve deep at the thickest, a great grey mass gleaming with steel, filling the dry watercourse. In the same twinkling of an eye I saw also that our right overlapped their left, that my troops would just strike the edge of their array, and that the troop on my right would charge into air. My subaltern comrade on the right, Wormald of the 7th Hussars, could see the situation too; and we both increased our speed to the very fastest gallop and curved inwards like the horns of the moon. One really had not time to be frightened or to think of anything else but these particular necessary actions which I have described. They completely occupied mind and senses.

The collision was now very near. I saw immediately before me, not ten yards away, the two blue men who lay in my path. They were perhaps a couple of yards apart. I rode at the interval between them. They both fired. I passed through the smoke conscious that I was unhurt. The trooper immediately behind me was killed at this place and at this moment, whether by these shots or not I do not know. I checked my pony as the ground began to fall away beneath his feet. The clever animal dropped like a cat four or five feet down on to the sandy bed of the watercourse, and in this sandy bed I found myself surrounded by what seemed to be dozens of men. They were not thickly packed enough at this point for me to experience any actual collision with them. Whereas Grenfell's troop, next but one on my left, was brought to a complete standstill and suffered very heavy losses, we seemed to push our way through as one has sometimes seen mounted policemen break up a crowd. In less time than it takes to relate, my pony had scrambled up the other side of the ditch. I looked round.

Once again I was on the hard, crisp desert, my horse at a trot. I had the impression of scattered Dervishes running to and fro in all directions. Straight before me a man threw himself on the ground. The reader must remember that I had been trained as a cavalry soldier to believe that if ever cavalry broke into the mass of infantry, the latter would be at their mercy. My first idea therefore was that the man was terrified. But simultaneously I saw the gleam of his curved sword as he drew it back for a hamstringing cut. I had room and time enough to turn my pony out of his reach, and leaning over on the off side I fired two shots into him at about three yards. As I straightened myself in the saddle, I saw before me another figure with uplifted sword. I raised my pistol and fired. So close were we that the pistol itself actually struck him. Man and sword disappeared below and behind me. On my left, ten yards away, was an Arab horseman in a bright-coloured tunic and steel helmet, with chain-mail hangings. I fired at him. He turned aside. I pulled my horse into a walk and looked around again.

In one respect a cavalry charge is very like ordinary life. So long as you are all right, firmly in your saddle, your horse in hand, and well armed, lots of enemies will give you a wide berth. But as soon as you have lost a stirrup, have a rein cut, have dropped your weapon, are wounded, or your horse is wounded, then is the moment when from all quarters enemies rush upon you. Such was the fate of not a few of my comrades in the troops immediately on my left. Brought to an actual standstill in the enemy's mass, clutched at from every side, stabbed at and hacked at by spear and sword, they were dragged from their horses and cut to pieces by the infuriated foe. But this I did not at the time see or understand. My impressions continued to be sanguine. I thought we were masters of the situation, riding the enemy down, scattering them and killing them. I pulled my horse up and looked about me. There was a mass of Dervishes about forty or fifty yards away on my left. They were huddling and clumping themselves together, rallying for mutual protection. They seemed wild with excitement, dancing about on their feet, shaking their spears up and down. The whole scene seemed to flicker. I have an impression, but it is too fleeting to define, of brown-clad Lancers mixed up here and there with this surging mob. The scattered individuals in my immediate neighbourhood made no attempt to molest me. Where was my troop? Where were the other troops of the squadron? Within a hundred yards of me I could not see a single officer or man. I looked back at the Dervish mass. I saw two or three riflemen crouching and aiming their rifles at me from the fringe of it. Then for the first time that morning I experienced a sudden sensation of fear. I felt myself absolutely alone. I thought these riflemen would hit me and the rest devour me like wolves. What a fool I was to loiter like this in the midst of the enemy! I crouched over the saddle, spurred my horse into a gallop and drew clear of the *mêlee*. Two or three hundred yards away I found my troop already faced about and partly formed up.

The other three troops of the squadron were reforming close by. Suddenly in the midst of the troop up sprang a Dervish. How he got there I do not know. He must have leaped out of some scrub or hole. All the troopers turned upon him thrusting with their lances: but he darted to and fro causing for the moment a frantic commotion. Wounded several times, he staggered towards me raising his spear. I shot him at less than a yard. He fell on the sand, and lay there dead. How easy to kill a man! But I did not worry about it. I found I had fired the whole magazine of my Mauser pistol, so I put in a new clip of ten cartridges before thinking of anything else.

I was still prepossessed with the idea that we had inflicted great slaughter on the enemy and had scarcely suffered at all ourselves. Three or four men were missing from my troop. Six men and nine or ten horses were bleeding from spear thrust or sword cuts. We all expected to be ordered immediately to charge back again. The men were ready, though they all looked serious. Several asked to be allowed to throw away their lances and draw their swords. I asked my second sergeant if he had enjoyed himself. His answer was 'Well, I don't exactly say I enjoyed it, Sir; but I think I'll get more used to it next time.' At this the whole troop laughed.

But now from the direction of the enemy there came a succession of grisly apparitions; horses spouting blood, struggling on three legs, men staggering on foot, men bleeding from terrible wounds, fish-hook spears stuck right through them, arms and faces cut to pieces, bowels protruding, men gasping, crying, collapsing, expiring. Our first task was to succour these; and meanwhile the blood of our leaders cooled. They remembered for the first time that we had carbines.

Everything was still in great confusion. But trumpets were sounded and orders shouted, and we all moved off at a trot towards the flank of the enemy. Arrived at a position from which we could enfilade and rake the watercourse, two squadrons were dismounted and in a few minutes with their fire at three hundred yards compelled the Dervishes to retreat. We therefore remained in possession of the field. Within twenty minutes of the time when we had first wheeled into line and began our charge, we were halted and breakfasting in the very watercourse that had so nearly proved our undoing. There one could see the futility of the much-vaunted *Arme Blanche*. The Dervishes had carried off their wounded, and the corpses of thirty or forty enemy were all that could be counted on the ground. Among them lay the bodies of over twenty Lancers, so hacked and mutilated as to be mostly unrecognizable. In all out of 310 officers and men the regiment had lost in the space of about two or three minutes five officers and sixty-five men killed and wounded, and 120 horses – nearly a quarter of its strength.

The Royal Navy, although the elimination of patronage proceeded no faster than the elimination of purchase in the army, developed much earlier an adequate system of professional education. The navy, however, had never suffered to anything like the same degree as the British army under the burden of class restriction on entry. It was in reference to the army that the Duke of Cambridge said in the 1850s: 'The British officer should be a gentleman first and an officer second.'[67] The very circumstances of a naval officer's occupation set a high premium upon competence in the furtherance of his career. This was not entirely free from the effect of social origins and connection, even after the introduction of limited competition for officer entry in 1820, and the reduction of the captain's powers of nomination in 1848. But the naval officer's career was never dominated by influence to the same extent as that of an officer in the army. The professional competence of the Royal Navy was rated the world over as very high and its prestige was enormous.

The growth of professionalism in the army in America was also retarded, even more so in fact than in England. The framers of the constitution were opposed to it. 'I am not acquainted with the military profession,' said one of them.[68] The constitution represented a liberal outlook to which the acceptance of a requirement for armed force was repugnant. Washington in his farewell address as Fraunces' Tavern advised that the nation should be able to 'choose peace or war as our interest guided by justice shall counsel'. But the last chance of the development of any significant degree of military professionalism in America for many years disappeared with the failure of the conservative federalism of Hamilton.

Something that the American sociologist Huntington calls military technicism[69] took its place. Each officer was expected to be expert in some speciality which he shared with civilians, while the body of military expertness which he shared only with other officers remained small. At the same time Jefferson's concept prevailed of a militia nation, in which a standing army all but disappeared. This contributed to a state of affairs in which professional military institutions, in so far as they were military, were very little developed by the time of the civil war. Even West Point, which Jefferson founded in 1802, and which exercised a formative influence over technical education in America, taught little of the liberal arts and almost nothing of military science. 'It produced,' in Huntington's words, 'more railroad presidents than generals.'

The Jacksonian period of liberal indifference to military affairs which followed ensured that while there should be no effective standing army there should be no efficient militia either. Promotion was only by seniority. In the army there was no retirement system until the civil war. Army officers served till they dropped. There were only three ranks in the navy with only two promotions in a lifetime. It is scarcely surprising that even the British system of promotion by purchase was felt by some to be preferable.

The American civil war, of far-reaching importance for the development of warfare, left the profession of arms in the United States at even lower ebb. The only significant support American military professionalism had ever received, that from the South, now dried up. Business pacifism reduced the army to a body of frontier police. This was actively enough engaged it is true (there were 943 engagements with Indians between the civil war and the end of the century), but the American army as a professional body was isolated, reduced and rejected.

American Civil War: tent life of 31st (82nd) Infantry at Queen's Farm near Fort Slocum, D.C., 1861

128

Paradoxically enough, the isolation of the military was the chief prerequisite to the development of professionalism. Withdrawn from civilian society and turning inwards upon themselves, the armed forces came under the influence of creative reformers like Sherman, Upton and Luce, followed by Bliss, Young, Carter and others in the army, Mahan, Taylor, Fiske in the navy. They looked abroad for most of their ideas.

General Upton's report on the organization, tactics and discipline of the armies of Europe and Asia made for General Sherman and Secretary Belknap in 1875, with especial reference to Germany, is a valuable mirror of the state of the military profession outside the United States.

The years between 1860 and the First World War saw the emergence of a distinctive American professional military ethic, with the American officer regarding himself as a member no longer of a fighting profession only, to which anybody might belong, but as a member of a profession which, if not accepted as learned, could still be intellectually demanding, and one whose students were students for life. With this view went the acceptance of the inevitability of conflict, arising out of the unchanging nature of man, and the consequent certainty of war. Norman Angell's view in *The Great Illusion* that, because war no longer paid, it was unlikely that any nation would go to war met sharp criticism. It treated man only as an economic animal and disregarded other causes of conflict.

Officers of the 114th Pennsylvania Infantry before Petersburg, Virginia, August 1864

1 September 1870.
Downfall of the Third
Empire: capitulation of
the French after Sedan

As the nineteenth century drew to a close professionalism in the armed services was everywhere to a greater or less degree apparent. Germany led the field. Prussian military efficiency was the path to national unity, through the unsuccessful war of 1848 in Denmark, the successful expansion of 1864, the victory of 1866 over Austria and the overthrow of France in 1870–1. France, shocked out of her post-Napoleonic apathy and even out of an antipathy to the military which sprang from a bourgeois uneasiness that standing armies could defeat or modify civil purposes, set about putting her professional military institutions in order.

The United States, as I have said, had evolved with remarkable speed a coherent system of military professionalism. England pursued a path of her own with a professional navy and a small regular army whose officers contained a high proportion of what by any criteria could only be described as amateurs drawn almost exclusively from a ruling caste. In one important respect, however, it was Britain that led the field. Nowhere else had civilian control over powerful armed forces been so effectively and easily established.

A further important development in the ordered application of force as a requirement of government had also taken place in the nineteenth century. This was the clear recognition of the function of police forces as distinct from the military, and their increase and reorganization to meet the newly formulated demands upon them. This happened very clearly in England with Sir Robert Peel's creation of a police force in 1829.

It is the function of police to exercise force, or to threaten it, in the execution of the state's purpose, internally and under normal conditions. It is the function of armed forces to exercise force, or the threat of it, externally in normal times and internally only in times which are abnormal. 'Law without force,' says Pascal, 'is impotent.'[70] The London policeman has until recently been almost always unarmed and usually urbane; the New York cop has always carried a gun; but the degree of force which the state is prepared to apply in the execution of its purpose is little different in England from that found in the United States. It is as much as the government of the day considers necessary or expedient to use to avoid a breakdown in its function and a surrender of its responsibilities.

When individuals or small groups act in a manner which the community has previously identified as intolerable they are restrained, or seized and made answerable if it has not been possible to restrain them. 'The existence of civilized communities,' says Bertrand Russell, 'is impossible without some element of force. When force is unavoidable it should be exercised by the constituted authority and in accordance with the will of the community.'[71]

British troops in Londonderry in 1972, observing a one-minute silence in respect to thirteen people killed on the previous Sunday in one of the more tragic misunderstandings which have darkened the Northern Irish scene

Belfast, 21 March 1972: after a bomb from the I.R.A. had killed six and injured 146 in a crowded shopping street, British soldiers of the Parachute Regiment succour civilian casualties

As larger political units develop by the coming together of national groups, once potentially hostile, violence could still be used by one group against another. The business of the constituted authority would then be, as before, to apply force to restrain the parties, just as police are now used to restrain gang warfare. I quote Bertrand Russell again. 'There are issues as to which men will fight and when they arise no form of government can prevent civil war.' The experience of the British in Northern Ireland in the second half of the twentieth century, particularly in regard to the highly important but not universally recognized effort to prevent internal violence from turning into civil war, adds depth to this perception.

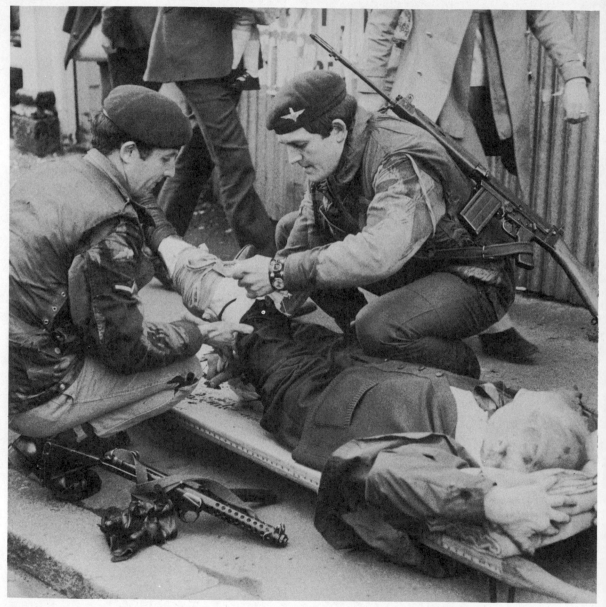

Let us return to the nation state. It is not surprising to find that the rate of advance in the professionalizing of armed forces has depended in each country on the degree to which national security is threatened or is thought to be. The impulse in Prussia which followed Jena weakened after the collapse of the Napoleonic threat. It quickened after the failure of Prussia against Denmark in 1848. In France the humiliation of 1815 was followed by acceleration in the development of professional military institutions, even though this was to slacken in an army from which conscription was temporarily removed by Louis XVIII and to which class restriction on entry into the officer establishment now returned. The French army remained nonetheless a professional body in the sense in which the army of Louis XV 100 years before had never been. Its performance in the Crimea was not particularly distinguished but that was a war which represented no real threat to national security. The French nation was not on the whole dissatisfied with its military forces in the mid-nineteenth century and did not seem greatly to desire anything more efficient.

The disaster of 1870 shocked the whole French nation into an urgent demand for reform. A wave of military professionalism followed, upon which France was to travel up to the First World War. In England the startling incompetence shown in the Crimea, and events about the same time in India, stimulated professionalism somewhat after 1856. The Prussian victory over France in 1870 was too sudden, too brutal and too close not to engender feelings of national insecurity in England with a further stimulus to professionalism as a consequence. The course and conduct of the South African war had a similar effect after 1902. But it was rather in the navy, upon which Britain's national security chiefly depended, that military professionalism in the country emerged. The army still had a long way to go.

The British army was still dominated by the principle that officers were gentlemen and non-officers were not, a principle which did no more than project the pattern of the parent society. Bernard Shaw tells the story of the gallant captain with the visiting card bearing, below his name, the legend 'The celebrated coward'. He had been a junior officer in the South African war. His superior had given him in battle an order which would have put success in the operation upon which they were engaged beyond a doubt. This would have meant his own probable promotion and the certain promotion of his superior. But the captain strongly believed that the British army should be officered only by gentlemen. His superior wasn't one. Therefore the captain ran away. He was cashiered of course, but he had ensured the failure of the operation and prevented forever the advancement of his superior. When this triumph of principle over self-interest was made known the captain was at once made an honorary member of several London clubs.

Though military professionalism developed at different rates in the Western world, conditions in the nineteenth century were generally favourable to its growth. They included a great increase in the complexity of military skills, the growing economic strength and competitiveness of the major nation states, the growth in power of the middle class at the

expense of landed aristocracy, and the development of democratic political institutions which demanded a more responsive articulation in armed forces. How far conscript service contributed to professionalism is obscure.

Huntington suggests a close link.[72] He argues that nationalism and democracy led to the concept of a nation in arms and thus to an army of conscript citizens. 'The shift in the officer corps from amateurism to professionalism,' he says, 'was virtually always associated with the shift in the rank and file from career soldiers to citizen soldiers.' Experience in his own country has not borne this out, nor has it in Great Britain. The shift to professionalism in the United States in the late nineteenth and early twentieth centuries preceded by a handsome margin the introduction of conscript service in the First World War. In the British army there was a significant development of professionalism in the 1930s. This preceded by only a few years the introduction of conscription in the Second World War, but it cannot be linked with it. As conscript national service faded out in Britain, professionalism in the services, instead of dwindling, began to increase.

The fact seems to be, to one who has served both in a conscript army in peace and war and in a voluntary army (which had its share of warfare) in peace, that in one important respect universal national service inhibits professionalism. Junior and middle-rank officers spend so much time and effort in the training of conscripts in elementary military skills that attention is to some extent withdrawn from the study of more advanced techniques.

Conscription tends to produce good soldier material, but this is only available for a short time in service. It probably reduces volunteer potential in the general community. It also probably makes it harder to build up a cadre of non-commissioned officers in the service. For the parent society conscript service is of high social significance. It is unfortunate when party political interests confuse this issue. Let us look at this question for a moment through French eyes.

Marshal Lyautey wrote an article in a French journal in 1891,[73] when universal military service had already been reintroduced in France, on the social role of the officer. National Service gave the nation a unique opportunity and the officer corps a heavy responsibility to society which was now no less moral than military. The officer's opportunity for service to society was now greater than any hitherto furnished by rare and fortuitous appearance on the battlefield. The young men of the nation were all being introduced at an impressionable age to an orderly life under the care of older men who, unlike the body of private industrial employers, did not draw financial profit from the labour of their workmen. The interests of both groups were not opposed. They were, or should be, the same. National service offered a vast field for social action. The officer should see himself as the educator of the nation.

I ask myself whether any nation has yet taken full advantage of the opportunities for social service offered by a system of universal military service. I used to feel that in Britain, though the moral and physical benefits of national service to very many young men were undoubted, we regular

Recruits to one of Her Majesty's five regiments of Foot Guards arrive at the depot on joining

In the cradle of the British Army: recruit instruction goes on at Aldershot after the Second World War

members of the service were not on the whole equal to the demands it made upon us. This was in part because we had been formed in a service whose function had been only that of defence, with no other additional purpose to be served. It was also because our masters in the state did not encourage us to find any other function in a national service army. The suggestion has been made in extenuation that there was little response to those officers who took their social duty to the men more seriously. When judgment is being passed upon a sculptor, however, arguments about the difficulty of working in stone carry little weight. The arguments for a long-service professional army are strong. But setting aside military considerations, the British have thrown away a great opportunity for social service

to the nation. Whether they would ever have used it, even if they had kept it, is another matter. They should at least make the best use of the very considerable opportunities which remain open to them, even in regular armed services.

I have one further point to raise. It is doubtful whether the unwritten clause of unlimited liability in the contract under which the man-at-arms engages to serve can easily be reconciled with conscript service. Of this contract I shall have a little more to say, as well as something of developments in warfare and their impact on the profession of arms in the twentieth century, in what follows.

Society and the Soldier 1914–18

I come now to the twentieth century, in which reflection upon the profession of arms soon compels us to face critical issues of our time. I do not wish at once to dwell upon the very grave dilemma created by the introduction into war of weapons of mass destruction, for this, though important, should not be allowed to obscure everything else. Before coming to it there is one thing I wish to say about the purpose of armed forces, the characteristics of armed service and of those who embrace it as a calling, and the relation of these institutions and men to their parent societies.

It is the business of armed services to furnish to a constituted authority, a government, in situations where force is or might be used, the greatest possible number of options. A government can have as many options as it will pay for. The greater the strength and variety, the better the equipment and training of its armed forces, the higher will be the number of options which will be open to it.

There are, of course, always limits to the amount any government will spend on defence. 'How great can the number of standing soldiers become,' asked a German critic of the 1780s, 'in comparison with the number of working subjects, before neither have anything to eat?'[74] This question arises today in somewhat different forms; it is the same question.

So long as sovereign states exist, however, the constituted authority of any one of them would be unwilling and unwise to abandon all power to direct the application of force in any situation where conflict between groups of men has resulted, or is likely to result, in violence. It must decide for itself, that is, how much it will spend and on what, how many and what sort of options it will pay for.

Now man normally lives in a group. He is a social animal, a πολιτικόν ζῷον.[75] The phrase is Aristotle's and the argument can be developed on something approaching Aristotelian lines. Anything can be called better or worse if it discharges a specific and distinguishing function more or less well. A good knife cuts well. A less good knife cuts less well. It is a distinguishing function of man, the political animal, to live in a society. The better able he is to do this, other things being equal, the better he is as a man. The better he is able to live in a city the more civilized he is, the more suited

First World War, London: Field Marshal Lord French, newly replaced as British C-in-C in France, reviews 10,000 volunteers before an enthusiastic crowd

Britain: an educated army in the making – the Army Service Corps Reading Room in Aldershot, 1900

to urban life, the more urbane, or, if you prefer the Greek, the better adapted to living in a polity, the politer. But living in a group demands some subordination of the interests of self to the interests of the group. The military contract stands out here as almost unique. It demands the total and almost unconditional subordination of the interests of the individual if the interests of the group should require it. This can lead to the surrender of life itself. It not infrequently does. Thus in an important respect the military would appear to be one of the more advanced forms of social institution.

This argument may appeal little to the average young officer. He might not actively reject it but would possibly find it of little relevance to what he is doing and why he supposes he is doing it. Since I believe, however, that it is not only now more important than ever before for intelligent men to join the military, but that it is the act of a rational man to do so, I am bound to set the argument out.

The military life is lived in order that an authority properly constituted over a significant group of men (such as a tribe, city, nation, state or federation) may be furnished with professional armed forces. If those bearing arms act in ways not consonant with the interests of the constituted authority, if they usurp its powers or dominate it, or in important ways put their own interests first, we have militarism. The proposition that militarism is suicidal has been described by Toynbee as 'almost a truism'.

But although militarism may be a suicidal perversion, though war may be bad, fighting may be bad, application of physical force among men may be bad (none of which is self-evidently true, but assuming it to be so), the military life, which would disappear if violence vanished among men, is in many important respects good.

Why this should be so is not difficult to see if we look at what have been called the military virtues. These, to quote an impartial witness in Toynbee, 'confront us as a monumental fact which cannot be whittled down or explained away'. But the military virtues are not in a class apart; 'they are virtues which are virtues in every walk of life . . . nonetheless virtues for being jewels set in blood and iron'.[76] They include such qualities as courage, fortitude and loyalty.

What is important about such qualities as these in the present argument is that they acquire in the military context, in addition to their moral significance, a functional significance as well. The essential function of an armed force is to fight in battle. Given equally advanced military techniques a force in which the qualities I have mentioned are more highly developed can confidently expect to defeat an equal force in which they are less and will often win when the opposing force is stronger. Thus while you may indeed hope to meet these virtues in every walk of life, and a good deal of educational effort is spent on developing them as being generally desirable, in the profession of arms they are functionally indispensable. The training, the group organizations, the whole pattern of life of the professional man-at-arms is designed in a deliberate effort to foster them, not just because they are morally desirable in themselves, but because they are essential to military efficiency. A digest of Cicero's *De Officiis* might well figure as a military training manual.

In consequence the moral tone in a military group tends to be higher than in a professional group where the existence of these qualities is desirable but not functionally essential, where their presence will make life for the members of the group more agreeable but will not necessarily make the group functionally more efficient. This is one reason why officers do not always find it easy at first to settle down and earn a living in civilian life, where the functional aspects of moral obligation are less apparent and the ex-officer is puzzled and sometimes distressed to find, for reasons he cannot always comprehend, a moral tone lower in some important respects than that to which he is accustomed.[77]

Mussolini said in the early 1930s: 'War alone brings all human energies to their highest tension, and sets a seal of nobility on the peoples who have the virtue to face it.'[78] This is rubbish, and dangerous rubbish at that. War does not ennoble. Kant's view that war has made more bad people than it has destroyed is probably nearer the mark.[79] But the interesting thing is that although war almost certainly does not ennoble, the preparation of men to fight in it almost certainly can and very often does.

British 'Volunteers', raised in 1859–60 against a threat of French invasion, the forerunners of today's Territorials

Men have joined armed forces at different times for different reasons.[80] I do not see many young men joining for the philosophical reasons I have suggested earlier, though I believe that reflections of the sort outlined then may help officers to realize the nature and the value of the life they lead. Almost always the desire for an active life has been prominent among reasons for taking up the profession of arms, but there have usually been contributory motives. These have often been ephemeral in value, and in kind accidental rather than essential. Sometimes the terms of reference have changed and disappointment has resulted.

Young Frenchmen of good family joined the armies of the *ancien régime* often because they had nothing else to do, or because it was expected of them, but very often also because of a real attachment to the concept of monarchy and some desire for distinction in the service of the king.

Young Prussian Junkers might be similarly motivated in entering the service of Frederick the Great. Frenchmen joined the revolutionary and Napoleonic armies on a surge of national spirit. Young Englishmen took commissions as Britain's empire grew, thinking that it was worthwhile doing something for the empire and hoping to have an interesting and exciting life, while they did it, into the bargain. They were not often disappointed. Young men in the United States, too, have joined one of the armed services to live an active and exacting life in an ordered society, whose purpose was to defend the values of a way of life they cherished.

Opposite: British infantry soldier on colonial service in 1890, with the new Lee Metford magazine rifle, the forerunner of the famous Lee-Enfield

R. Caton Woodville
1889

But the scene can change. Alfred de Vigny, of royalist family though he was, joined for *gloire* in Napoleon's time. Napoleon vanished into exile and *gloire* faded. De Vigny was left seeking a more enduring cause for the real satisfaction he and others about him derived from the soldier's life. He found it in abnegation. The British empire has dwindled too, swiftly and sharply, and not a few who joined the British armed forces when the sun still had not set on Government House found little comfort in the rising commonwealth, soon itself to dwindle.

I suppose there are some, in Western countries, who have become professional fighting men to fight Communism, though I rather hope not. I suppose there are some, in Eastern countries, who have become professional fighting men to fight Capitalism, though I hope that this is not so either. Certainly East–West divisions are likely to persist and if a young man has reasons such as these for joining armed forces today they are unlikely to go cold on him, like poor de Vigny's *gloire*.

Are reasons such as these valid, however, or do they suggest a faulty distribution of emphasis between essence and accident? I cannot help thinking that they do. Officers in the British service do not always fully understand their own reasons for taking the shilling, as they used to say, in reference to the token payment given the new recruit on his enlistment, and are happily reluctant to discuss the more important ones. I know one Oxford undergraduate who went on record in 1932 as saying that since a second world war was inevitable he would take a regular commission because he found it tidier to be killed as a professional than as an amateur. He was aware, he said, of the characteristic English argument that it was more elegant to be killed as an amateur, but he elected for the other option.

hope you will be glad to hear that this logically-minded man, though wounded now and then in the Second World War, is still very much alive today. He is the author of this text.

The military institution, however, is a persistent social form. The essential reasons which induce rational men to devote their adult lives to it, with its well-understood demands and accepted risks, are unlikely to be discreditable. Our difficulty here lies in identifying reasons of constant validity and separating them from others of temporary and often, it seems to me, dubious worth: any officer who honestly tries to do this will not, I think, be disillusioned.

I want to take up the thread again now at the point I reached earlier on, in giving an account of the rise of professionalism in Europe at the beginning of the twentieth century.

On the ground in Europe at that time the chief powers had 4 million men under arms, eight times the numbers in the early eighteenth century. Before long they would mobilize nearly ten times as many.

Now wars are not started by military commanders. De Tocqueville said more than a century ago, 'In a political democracy the most peaceful of all people are the generals.'[81] Events since then suggest that this may be true under other forms of government as well. The advice given by the German general staff to the Kaiser before the First World War, for example, was on the cautious side. Hitler's generals received the *Führer*'s proposals for a war against France, a quarter of a century later, with little enthusiasm and his subsequent willingness to accept a war on two fronts with dismay. In no country are the professional men-at-arms less likely than in Britain, where civilian control has become by evolution pretty well complete, to push the

First World War: German infantry advance in winter

country into war. In the United States, which is second only to Britain ɪ the length of time it has been governed under the same constitution, in spite of all that is said about the power of the military–industrial complex, the generals are scarcely more likely to drive the country into war than they are in Britain.

Even when a war has begun, it is still the politicians who play the biggest part in conducting it. But whatever responsibilities the politicians may have to bear, the social consequences of intellectual inadequacy in high military command have in this century already been appalling.

While the French were ordering national defence with the urgency born of their recent humiliation by Prussia, a new and visionary trend in military thinking began to appear in France. There were protests against a materialistic view of war. Nietzsche had already raised them in Germany. Writers like Ardant du Picq echoed and developed them in France, and evoked wide response when they spoke of the spirituality of war. Clausewitz had already urged the sovereign virtues of the will to conquer and the unique value of the offensive delivered with unlimited violence. A military voluntarism began to develop in France. When General Colin emphasized the importance of material factors he was laughed at. The business of the intellect was to overcome and rule out all consideration of losses, to bring about a disregard of all material obstacles to the offensive.

Engels was one of those who knew better than to underrate material factors: 'Force is no mere act of will but calls for . . . tools . . . the producer of more perfect tools, *vulgo* arms, beats the producer of more imperfect ones.'[82]

Already by 1894 the basis of all French tactics was once more the mass attack. Foch, who became head of the Ecole de Guerre in 1908, taught that the tactical fact of battle is the only argument in war and that battle demands, above all, offensive action *à outrance*.[83] The French army, said Grandmaison in 1912, more extreme even than Foch and (in Liddell Hart's words) the precipitator of disaster in 1914, no longer knows any other law than the offensive, which can only be carried through at the expense of bloody sacrifice.[84]

Napoleon had said in 1805, 'All my care will be to gain victory with the least shedding of blood.' How far he may have meant what he said is doubtful. But Napoleon was only quoted by the French military in the 1900s when he was useful and this observation was ignored.

The impact of modern techniques was misunderstood or disregarded. In the eighty years between Clausewitz and 1911 the rate of rifle fire had increased from three rounds per minute to sixteen, the range of guns from 1,000 yards to 5–6,000. Of artillery one responsible French officer said, 'We have rather too much of it.'[85] Arrangements for ammunition even for what there was failed to take into account 'the appetites of quick-firing guns'. In spite of the experiences of the American civil war Foch argued that a greater volume of small-arms fire favoured the attack. Of aviation and 'all that sport', he said, 'it's zero'.[86] After the war was over Foch was to say, 'We then believed morale alone counted, which is an infantile notion.' Before it, the elderly theorist who had never been in a major battle taught

His Imperial Majesty William II, Emperor of Germany and King of Prussia, 1859–1941, the 'Kaiser' of the First World War. His later years, from the end of hostilities until his death, were spent in exile in Holland

147

American Civil War: Union Troops at the long drawn-out siege of Petersburg, 1864–5

that victory is won by a single supreme stroke at one point. Later, when he had himself risen to supreme command of the Allied armies on the Western Front and contributed more than any other single man to Allied victory, Foch was to say that 'victory is won by bits and scraps'. 'I have only one merit,' he said quite early on in the war, 'I have forgotten what I taught, and what I learned.'[87]

From the very outset, however, in 1914, the French were totally committed to a policy of attack. General Joffre, the Commander-in-Chief, pressed on under what was known as Plan XVII with an all-out offensive eastwards in Lorraine. He had plenty of evidence that the Germans were doing exactly what the general he had replaced was dismissed for saying they would do, that is, enveloping the French northern flank. He disregarded this and pressed on to the east.

The offensive in Lorraine failed. Within three weeks the French had been thrown back everywhere with the loss of 300,000 men and the Germans were threatening Paris. Plan XVII was in ruins and with it the French pre-war army. Very soon and for the rest of the war the Western Front was dominated, as the Russo-Japanese war had already indicated would probably happen, by entrenchment, barbed wire and bullets from automatic weapons.[88]

As the First World War dragged on, French devotion to the all-out offensive died hard. Many men died with it, often fighting only to gain ground in accordance with the sterile doctrine that ground, simply in and for itself, gave an advantage. The French dead in the First World War amounted to nearly one-and-a-half million. Four-and-a-half million were wounded. Three-quarters of the 8 million men mobilized in France were casualties. They were mostly young men. The memorial tablet in the chapel of the French officer-cadet school at St Cyr, destroyed in the Second World War, contained one single entry for 'The Class of 1914'.[89] The population of France had not doubled between Valmy and the Marne[90] but the number of lives lost in defending the Ile-de-France had been increased one hundredfold. The social results to the nation of these losses, which make themselves more powerfully felt as time goes by, are still incalculable. They cannot fail in the aggregate to be enormous.

Very many of these deaths were the direct consequence not only of failures in management and faults of technique but also of error in the formulation of general principles. The French came into the First World War the slaves of an abstract military concept which was totally invalid but from which they only painfully struggled free.

Following pages: First World War. British troops over the top in the costly Somme offensive, July 1916

Western Front 1914: German infantry in the advance. Such close formations invited heavy casualties

U.S. soldier, 1918

The British also made costly errors, not so much of abstract thought as of practical applications. The Commander-in-Chief in 1914, Field Marshal French, was a cavalryman like many other senior commanders in the First World War, including Douglas Haig, who was first a corps commander and then the Field Marshal's successor as Commander-in-Chief. Both French and Haig had shown marked ability as administrators, trainers and commanders of troops, with distinguished records in the South African war. Neither had the intellectual capacity to evaluate the importance of new techniques, or the imagination to break the bonds of his own experience.

French was often quite plainly out of his depth, besides being a little suspicious of his allies. '*Au fond*, they are a low lot,' he wrote, 'one always has to remember the class these French generals mostly come from.'[91] Both he and Haig planned to use large masses of cavalry in exploitation of infantry success, even when conditions on the Western Front had long condemned mounted troops, used as such, either to idleness, in a phrase of Michael Howard's, or suicide. Ian Hamilton had reported from the Russo-Japanese war, when bullet, wire and trench became dominant, that the only

Opposite: First World War. French graves at Douamont, Verdun

153

Left: Cloudless May.
General Weygand
inspects the preparation of
French defensive
positions in the
Somme-Aisne area in
1940

Right: The German
offensive of March 1918
nears its end: reserve
troops in trenches

Below: France 1918. A
wounded American
soldier, revolver in hand,
guards a disabled officer
until help comes

First World War: British infantry moving up into the line after the savage setback at Loos in 1915

use for cavalry there had been to cook rice for the infantry, but he was thought by some to be insane. Haig had said earlier on that artillery was only effective against demoralized troops. He had written in a minute to the Army Council in April 1915 that the machine-gun was a much over-rated weapon, and two per battalion were more than sufficient.[92] The number was fortunately increased a little later on to eight and then, largely on civilian pressure, to sixteen.

Examples could be multiplied of the failure of the professionals to realize the 'terrible transformation in the character of war which,' says Toynbee, '. . . took our generation by surprise in 1914.'[93]

The sad tale of what occurred on the second day of the battle of Loos is probably worth choosing here as an example of what could happen.

Two new British infantry divisions were committed on the morning of 26 September 1915 to the continuation of a mass attack on German positions, of which the front lines had been penetrated the day before. The barbed wire of the reserve positions was heavy and intact. For the British

...ack there was nothing that could be called artillery preparation. Twenty minutes of desultory shell fire, which appears to have caused the Germans no casualties, was followed by a pause of about half an hour. Then twelve battalions, 10,000 men, on a clear morning, in columns, advanced up a gentle slope towards the enemy's trenches. The wire behind which these lay was still unbroken.

The British advance met with a storm of machine-gun fire. Incredulous, shouting in triumph, the Germans mowed the attackers down until, three-and-a-half hours later, the remnants staggered away from the 'Leichenfeld von Loos', having lost 385 officers and 7,861 men. The Germans, as they watched the survivors leave, stopped firing in compassion. Their casualties in the same time had been nil.

> 'Good-morning; good-morning!' the General said
> When we met him last week on our way to the line.
> Now the soldiers he smiled at are most of 'em dead,
> And we're cursing his staff for incompetent swine.
> 'He's a cheery old card,' grunted Harry to Jack
> As they slogged up to Arras with rifle and pack.
> But he did for them both with his plan of attack.[94]

It is not only the battle of Loos which these lines of Siegfried Sassoon, written in 1917, call to mind. The lives at Loos were thrown away. Nothing was gained at all except a painful lesson we could do without. But there are many other occasions in four years of war which included Neuve Chapelle, the Somme, the battles around Ypres and Passchendaele, when inadequacy in command caused grievous loss of life for no return. The total of British dead was around the million mark. Casualties were about half those in France where the productive and creative capacity of a whole generation was pretty well taken clean out. The social historian of the future is likely to find the results in both cases significant.

Let us not minimize the responsibilities of others besides the military commanders, but these have much to bear. In the examples I have chosen the French and the British each made cardinal errors in spheres which were peculiarly their own, the French in their failure to evolve a valid concept, the British in their failure to evaluate current techniques.

These generals were not all wicked men nor always stupid men and they were very rarely cowards. Their errors were more those of blindness than malignity. Where they failed was in understanding the techniques of their time. In consequence they could not formulate sound principles and their handling was faulty. Sometimes, as in Foch's case, they found they had to modify radically in practice what they once had preached. Whatever their many good qualities they were often unequal to their task, and when they made mistakes the results were often appalling, with the most serious consequences for Western society.

What thought, in our own society in Britain, to speak of what I know best, was given in the late nineteenth and early twentieth century to preventing these mistakes? The army was left largely where it was. Its

other-rank personnel was improving, with a rising standard of living, but its officer corps was still the preserve of young men of good social standing who had the outlook of amateurs, which is what they mostly were. They were ill-paid, with 'half a day's pay for half a day's work', and so had to be of independent means. This meant that most were hard to teach and many were unteachable. They were not well trained and were expected to be neither industrious nor particularly intelligent. From men such as these came the commanders of the First World War. As a foreign observer put it, among the officers of the British army bravery had often to compensate for lack of ability.[95]

What a society gets in its armed services is exactly what it asks for, no more and no less. What it asks for tends to be a reflection of what it is. When a country looks at its fighting forces it is looking in a mirror; the mirror is a true one and the face that it sees will be its own.

First World War: a wounded prisoner in the battle of the Somme, 1916

Today and Tomorrow

After the First World War there was a tendency in the military behaviour of victor states to revert to earlier patterns. 'I hate wars,' a Russian Archduke once said. 'They spoil the armies.' In 1919 'real soldiering', as they put it in the British Army, was now back again. The Russians, of course, were then busy with their revolution, and the painful birth pangs of a child of high promise doomed in the fullness of time to dreadful deformity. The Turkish and Austro-Hungarian empires had come apart. The Arabs were awakening from a long sleep while in Europe a patchwork of succession states came into being under pressure from starry-eyed Americans persuaded that ethnic entity was sacred and self-determination an over-riding requirement. Germany was trying to cope with the grim realities of total defeat in war, under the delusion that she had been tricked into it. France was facing a long convalescence after the monstrous blood-letting which had virtually destroyed a generation. Britain picked up her old imperial role again, unable to believe it would not last for ever, while some other European countries, France prominent among them, also did much the same. The United States withdrew into international semi-isolation from a world upon much of which she had imposed a fragile new order, with a League of Nations she at once abandoned. Fertilized by British rejection of a continental security commitment the seeds of another war had been already sown.

In spite of the return in Britain to proper soldiering and the imperial image, the United Kingdom in the 1930s was already building a better and more modern army. Professionalism, though still unwelcome in the better regiments, was creeping in. With mechanization and above all in armoured warfare Britain was ahead of the field. The notion that peacetime soldiering was an agreeable and gentlemanly pastime for an ill-paid amateur of independent means died hard and has never perhaps entirely disappeared. The 1930s, however, saw a radical change, of which one of the most startling single manifestations was that regimental officers now worked not only in the morning but in the afternoon as well. They were also more generously paid, given better promotion prospects and required to

Vietnam: a U.S. Marine of H Company, Second Battalion, Fifth Marines carries a wounded comrade to an evacuation landing zone in the last stages

161

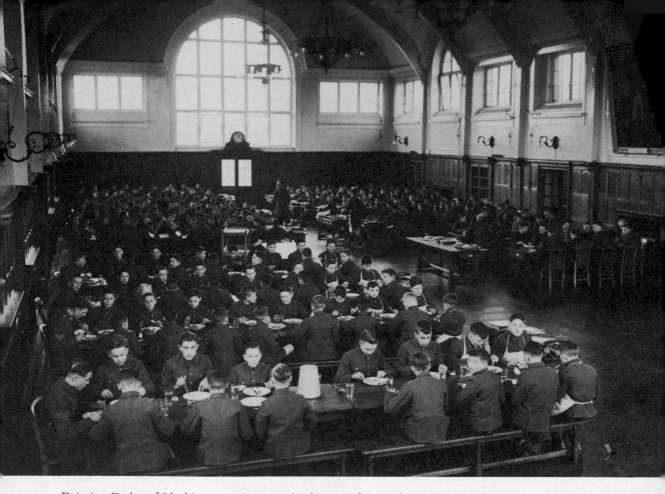

Britain: Duke of York's School. Dinner-time, with some of the boys in aprons fresh from Carpentry Class

conform to higher professional standards. It is almost certainly true that Britain's refusal to put the claims of international security in Europe above those of her overseas empire was a major cause of the Second World War, as well as of the reverses encountered in its early stages. British armed services at its outbreak, however, were as professionally competent as any in the world, under commanders who, once the second-raters found at the beginning of any war had been replaced, were on the whole a good deal better than those of the First World War. The dissolution of Empire since the end of the Second World War has concentrated the military mind in Britain wonderfully. British defence forces today, in the closing decades of the twentieth century, are undoubtedly better than they have ever been before, enjoying as well an enviably smooth and stable relationship with the society they serve. They can make a good claim, size apart, to be the best of any nation in the world.

Before we move too far from the Second World War reflection upon it inevitably invites judgment on the quality of professional performance in the chief contenders. There is no doubt at all about who wins first prize. It is the Germans. An army's good qualities are best shown when it is losing. The choice of title for the memoirs of an outstanding German field commander in the Italian Campaign of 1944–5, when the war was already lost and most people knew it, really says it all. General von Senger und Etterlin called his book *Without Hope and Without Fear*.

I had abundant experience myself, from the other side, of the high competence of German command and the responsiveness of the machine it handled, none remembered more vividly than what happened in Operation 'Market Garden', the Allied Anglo-American airborne attempt to open a way into Germany and end the war in September 1944. Some of our own commanders and staff, who may have had less first-hand experience of fighting Germans than others, thought that since defences were weak in the area round Arnhem we in the First British Airborne Division could expect to seize fairly easily a bridgehead across the lower Rhine there, and hold it long enough for Allied ground troops to get up to us. Older hands, who had seen the swiftness and violence of German reaction to a threat to anything that really mattered, were not so sanguine. Our operation failed. The response of the most highly effective army the world has yet seen saw to that. In the four months I spent myself in hiding with brave Dutch people after the battle, recovering from wounds received in it, there was ample time to reflect on this. The Germans in the Second World War were very, very good, from Norway to Sicily, from France to Stalingrad, from Normandy to North Africa. Wherever they fought they were on the

Royal Military Academy, Sandhurst: cadets fencing

163

1944: German photograph of British dead at Arnhem

whole well commanded and well disciplined and for the most part, with exceptions little found in the regular army, well behaved. A question for the Western Alliance in the late twentieth century is how far the quality and performance of the German army in the Second World War is likely to be reflected in the Bundeswehr of the Federal Republic. The signs are not unpromising.

It has, in our time, been customary to think of war and peace as though these are mutually exclusive conditions, as though you must be at war if you are not at peace and vice versa. This is hardly self-evident and certainly untrue at any time when war is not total, as it was not in the mid-eighteenth century. When Sterne set out from England on his Sentimental Journey in 1762 he had forgotten that England was at war with France. He had no passport and was given one at Versailles by, as it was said, the Foreign Minister himself, who was then actively prosecuting the Seven Years War against England. '*Un homme qui rit*,' said the Minister, '*ne sera jamais dangereux.*'[96] When England and France were in a state of war most people continued to be unaffected, and very many would never even have heard about it at all.

All that changed with the French Revolution and Napoleon's unmannerly intrusion into a world of limited war.[97] Through the nineteenth century, even in times of deceptive peace, forms of political thought and of professional military practice continued to develop along lines leading straight towards total national war.

We owe a great deal here to the Germans. The response to the Napoleonic challenge, which had led to the collapse of Jena, was the overhaul of German military institutions followed by the development of a national frame, strongly influenced by the teaching of Hegel, in which to house them. The movement towards national unity and absolute sovereignty gathered strength as the Prussian army became more formidable.

General Montgomery, seen here with Major-General Urquhart (G.O.C. First British Airborne Division) and Brigadier Hackett, visits the 4th Parachute Brigade at Oakham, England, in early 1944

A military philosophy, that of Clausewitz, appeared just when it was most wanted. The Germany of our time was founded in war in the nineteenth century and tested in war as the century progressed. Bismarck's three wars of Prussian aggression established the German state as we came to know it in the twentieth century. It would be a gross error to hold Germany entirely responsible for the two great world catastrophes of the first half of this century, but it is undeniable that both revolved around Germany as the central figure.

Just as the last of these two world wars ended, the missing piece dropped into place and the pattern was complete; the concept of total war between sovereign national states was now matched with a technique of total destruction.

As a result, if by war we still mean total war, as Clausewitz did, war can no longer be what Clausewitz called it – the continuation of policy by other means. It is difficult to argue, though I know some do (for example Herman Kahn in *On Thermonuclear War*), that unrestricted war between powers of high and roughly equal nuclear capability can possibly be brought about by a rational act of deliberate policy. General war can result, it seems to me, from miscalculation or abberration or mischance. It just possibly might come back into play as a rational act of policy, for a short time, in the very unlikely event of a radical technical advance which gives one power an overwhelming, if temporary, superiority over the rest. War in the sense of general unrestricted war, however, can no longer be regarded as a normal continuation of foreign policy or an alternative to peace.

It is of vital importance here to recognize the dangerous and probably suicidal folly of a supposition by any superpower that it can 'win', or even 'survive', in any acceptable sense of the term, an unrestricted nuclear war with another. It is the tacit acceptance of this that probably did more than anything else to ensure decades of peace in Europe after the Second World War, while two hugely armed power blocs confronted each other across indefensible land frontiers in deep and bitter hostility.

On the other hand it would be quite unrealistic to suppose that the unlikelihood of general nuclear war will reduce the probability of warfare at a lower level. Its prevalence outside Europe in those very same decades, when at least forty identifiable wars took place in less than forty years with more than forty million dead, suggests the reverse. The inevitability of warfare in the foreseeable future has to be accepted as a fact of life, no less evident than the vital necessity to prevent any war from becoming a nuclear war. The need to avoid warfare where this is possible and to contain it when it is not will throw a great and growing burden upon the military professional as time goes by. The world approaches one of the most dangerous periods in its history as the ownership of nuclear weapons spreads among lesser powers.

What has the introduction of nuclear weapons done to the profession of arms? I would say its most significant effect is to emphasize the importance of bringing in the best people. The greater the danger, and the more urgently it threatens, the higher the quality of person required in the profession, and the greater the need for confidence between the soldier and the society he serves. War was once a game – a dangerous and a lethal game whose result could be critical to the interests or even the survival of the loser, but a game nonetheless, in which the players were only a small part of the human group they represented. It then became total, engaging the interest and demanding the participation of practically every member of any nation state involved. It has now developed into a potential threat to mankind's life on earth. There have been advances in warlike method before now which have aroused acute disquiet. The crossbow was regarded by many as an instrument of the devil, to be banned by Christian folk. The introduction of explosives was seen by many more as a clear indication that warfare had become so destructive that it must now stop. Techniques have multiplied since then, of which some, such as the development of steam propulsion, automatic fire, the internal combustion engine, aviation and electronics, to choose only a few, have enormously increased the lethal and destructive power of armed forces. Warfare has gone on unchecked. Nuclear weapons represent the latest and by far the greatest quantum jump in military technology since one man first brandished a club or threw a stone at another. This will not stop men fighting. What we know is that when men fight, the fighting must not involve the use of nuclear weapons if mankind is to survive. How this prevention is to be contrived is perhaps (though there are many other claimants to priority such as world-wide pollution, the exhaustion of irreplaceable natural resources and starvation in the Third World) the most important issue of our time. However it is approached the professional man-at-arms will have a critical position in its resolution.

Unfortunately we are often the prisoners of terms like 'war' and 'peace'. Forms of national organization are still closely related to this outworn dichotomy. In the Western world, certainly in Western Europe and the United States, much legislation and many administrative arrangements (particularly those relating to the armed forces) are only comprehensible in terms of it. Confusion and inefficiency readily result.

What is required (in addition to whatever preparations may be thought necessary for total war) is the ability to deploy that degree of warlike effort which the circumstances demand, in gentle graduation from something very small to something which, though pretty large, is still short of general mobilization. This is more easily contrived in the United States than in Britain which is still burdened with a system distinguishing between war and peace, on the assumption that each is an identifiable and uniform state excluding the other. To this the British have made a few makeshift adjustments. But they are still far from a smoothly working concept of partial war and partial peace in varying degrees of either.

For people who have brought so much benefit to the world by accident or absent-mindedness it is astonishing how prone the British have become in military affairs to seek triumphs of tidiness over commonsense. They are, of course, not alone in this tendency but they furnish outstanding examples of it. In considering desirable national force levels the men in Whitehall in the 1960s, for example, set out Britain's treaty obligations and against each

one what troops were required to meet it: four divisions for N.A.T.O., one in reserve at home, four battalions for this commitment overseas, three and a half for that and so on. When a treaty was due to lapse as time-expired the troop requirement was struck out of the estimates. The assumption was that you need hardly do more than provide for the predictable, though it must be clear that armed forces, like insurance policies, are chiefly of value as provision against the unknown. The householder is not required to identify the burglar in advance. Operations can become necessary in a quite unexpected way. The Falklands demonstrated that.

Tensions between men and the causes of conflict between sovereign states would not be lessened even if it were universally accepted that total war had disappeared entirely as a valid act of deliberate national policy.

Anti-military rally of 4,000 people calling for a ceasefire between Britain and Argentina in the Falkland Islands dispute march past the Cenotaph erected in Whitehall to honour the dead in two world wars

169

1982: British troops face stone-throwing rioters in Belfast

War, total war, we have to avoid. Warfare, acts of organized violence between groups of men which in sum amount to less than total war, which we are unlikely to be able entirely to prevent, we must do something about.

How do we avoid total war? One widely supported suggestion is that general war could not take place if we all agreed to do away with the means to wage it. General and complete disarmament is therefore put forward as the answer, perhaps with nuclear disarmament first. Others argue that, so long as sovereign states exist, no such agreements, even with far better guarantees than the great powers are at present likely to agree upon, can be foolproof. The argument goes as follows: there is now a high degree of transferability between civil and military skills. Since techniques cannot be abolished, an attempt to lock the weapons up or destroy them is not a very sensible way of trying to prevent conflict. An agreement for general and complete disarmament would probably raise more problems than it would solve. The prevention of total war, therefore, can probably best be approached through arms control.

It is evidence of widely spread concern over the danger of nuclear war that what has been described as the peace movement developed so strongly in the West in the early 1980s. The Soviet Union publicly claimed to have given this movement much material and moral support and there is no reason to doubt this, for while such manifestations could be (and were) easily suppressed in the U.S.S.R., their support in the West could only be to the Warsaw Pact's evident advantage. Such was the degree of concern in Western countries that even the most naive of suggestions received wide support if it were put forward as a genuine attempt at reduction of the risk of nuclear attack. It was proposed, for instance, to disarm on the Western side unilaterally, to set an example which would then be followed (presumably under pressure of public opinion) in the Warsaw Pact. Quite intelligent people often took this proposal quite seriously. 'Nuclear-free zones', declared on a national, regional or local level, were also proposed, on the principle that if where you lived there were no nuclear weapons you would be immune from nuclear attack. Few housewives bombed out in West Beirut in 1982 could have supposed that there was ever much guarantee of immunity from Israeli bombs in the absence of anti-aircraft weapons from that particular street. The only way to secure the British Isles from attack in an all-out East–West war would be to tow them somewhere else, which is a scarcely less realistic notion than some put forward by the nuclear disarmers.

1982: anti-cruise missile demonstrators outside the Law Courts in London

I mention these arguments not to take sides nor yet to poke fun at people of whom most were so deeply worried as to be readily misled. The point that has to be made is a rather obvious one. In the prevention of total war, whatever means are chosen, the state will continue to rely heavily upon the military professional. Neither a working system of arms control nor an effective state of general disarmament is possible without him.

Still less can you dispense with the military in the unlikely event that some discriminate form of nuclear warfare emerges. I hold it to be a dangerous illusion to believe that controlled or limited nuclear war is possible. The release of the first nuclear weapon on land will, in my own view, open Pandora's box and we cannot guess what will come out. What is all too likely to emerge is steep and early escalation into the total nuclear exchange we all dread. But allowing, for the sake of the argument, the possibility of controlled nuclear war, the search for the conditions under which it would take place, the study of it, its conduct if it were to come about, would make heavy demands on the capacity of military professionals.

French country folk place flowers on the body of an American soldier killed in front of their home at Carentan, France, June 1944, and offer a prayer

Short Blowpipe *hand-held supersonic anti-aircraft guided missile*

Even without nuclear weapons it must be admitted that warfare of some sort cannot be seen as anything but quite inevitable. No one can say in advance when or how armed conflict between groups of men will emerge. What goes on in the world at this moment offers no encouragement whatsoever to those who have hoped during the last few decades that the tendency to resort to armed conflict will decline.

Who will predict with any confidence what the pattern of violence may be in the next few years, or the next half-century? The mathematical resources of the social scientist may be of help here in the long run, but they are not yet sufficiently reliable to furnish much guidance to makers of policy. It is difficult to say how conflict will emerge or what form it will take. All we can say with confidence is that it will occur.

Edward Gibbon in the late eighteenth century predicted the early disappearance of warfare between nations.[98] He was wrong. The First World War was 'the war to end wars'. It was followed by the Second World War. The Third World War has to be prevented, if this is humanly possible, but that would make little if any difference to the tendency to minor outbreaks of violence, except perhaps to increase their frequency. For if you can take a club to your neighbour without bringing down a thunderbolt you will club him the more readily.

Now since fighting is bound to take place, situations are easily conceivable in which the only hope of avoiding something worse may lie in taking a hand in it. I believe we have already arrived at a position in which the main purpose of the profession of arms is not to win wars but to avoid them. This will almost certainly demand the taking of deliberate decisions to fight; that is to say, by embarking on timely warfare to lessen the risk of general war.

If this is so, the chief function of the armed forces maintained by properly constituted authorities, whether these are nation states or something else, now becomes the containment of violence. We may thus be moving towards what Janowitz has called a constabulary concept. Within such a concept the function and duty of the military professional remain the same. His function is the orderly application of armed force. His duty is to develop his skill in the management of violence to the utmost and to act in its exercise as the true subordinate of the properly constituted authority, whatever this may turn out to be.[99]

A situation can arise where military professionals themselves set up a national authority which then secures wider recognition, even if this is reluctantly given, and is thus legitimized. The junta is an all too frequent and unwelcome aberration in the twentieth century. It is unfortunately the case that when civil government breaks down, or is too weak to withstand strong action by ambitious men, armed forces are ideally constituted (and often most conveniently located) for the seizure of power. They have a structure designed to ensure the rapid and effective execution of orders from above. They have weapons, mobility, communications and discipline. The seizure of civil power is for the military often too temptingly easy. Its exercise is another matter, for which armed forces are neither intended nor apt. Its devolution is very difficult, which is even more serious. Transfer of power from an army comes about normally through defeat in battle and not through the ballot box. The military can easily seize power. They find it very hard to get rid of it once it has been secured.

England had her experience of military government in the seventeenth century, under a stern and selfless Christian, Oliver Cromwell, whose powers had resulted in the execution of the anointed King, Charles I. England, in the event, did not like it. The harmonious relationship between civil and military power, which has persisted in Britain since then, in which the subordination of the military to the civil is fundamental, owes much to this salutary experience.

It should be added here that total, blind, unquestioning obedience in any circumstances whatsoever must never be demanded of any human being. In the last resort a man is answerable to his own conscience for what he does, and nowhere else. He has to be prepared to say 'I will not' if his conscience tells him that he must, and take the consequences. These, in war, could be severe. A commander must do all he can to ensure that no man is put into a situation where he is bound, on grounds of conscience, to disobey. A man set under authority must be prepared to go to very great lengths indeed before he does so, recognizing that his disobedience will not only put himself at hazard but probably comrades too. He must above all be on his guard against manipulation by the ill-intentioned. Happily, commanders in national armies know, or should know, enough about the nature of the men they command to recognize where limits lie. I have known, in my service, of orders given and obeyed in other armies which I should for my own part have neither obeyed nor transmitted. I have never been asked in my own service to do anything that, on grounds of conscience, I could not.

Some minds are troubled by a misunderstanding of the sixth Commandment, which in the Authorized Version reads 'Thou shalt not kill' (*Exodus* chapter 20, verse 13). The misunderstanding melts away before the

study of judgments in the next two chapters. In these it is clear that in response to certain specified acts it is not merely permitted to take life: the law positively demands it. Thus the meaning of the Commandment is abundantly clear. What is condemned is killing when the law does not enjoin it, that is to say, murder. To take life at the direction of the properly constituted authority under which a society lives and is regulated is not only right; it can be a duty. The soldier's conscience is on this point perfectly clear, the more so since he usually offers his own life at least as often and as readily as he takes another's.

Engels drew attention to the close reflection of the dominant political characteristics of nineteenth-century states in their military establishments.[100] I have already suggested that this correspondence has not been confined to the nineteenth century. It is not only the political structure of a society but its social characteristics as well which are reflected in the pattern of its armed forces.

The pattern of society in Great Britain is evolving and the pattern of her armed forces will evolve in conformity with it, whether we like it or not. Some of an older generation possibly do not. They may like it as little as the Duke of Wellington liked the proposals to abolish purchase. But it is the business of those in responsible positions in a nation's armed forces today to see that modification of structure to correspond to a changing pattern in society is facilitated, while careful attention is paid to the preservation of what is worth preserving.

The traumatic experience of the United States in the war in Vietnam has received wide attention. Some would say it has received too much, and not always in ways that can be justified. Instant televisual reporting was perhaps inevitable but its effect, when emotional and political pressures in the

Washington: anti-Vietnam war protests outside the Pentagon on 21 October 1967

176

Infantryman from the South Vietnamese 7th Division, wounded in fighting on 14 January 1970, after withdrawal of the U.S. Ninth

United States were high and diverse, could hardly fail to do the U.S. Army grave disservice. The lack of sympathy widely generated in the American people towards its armed forces as a result of the war in Vietnam may still take time entirely to correct. The passage of some years since the war ended and the seizure of public interest in the meantime by other armed conflicts has already done much to correct it. This is not the time and place to add to the already large volume of comment and analysis in relation to this sad and readily misread affair. One very important aspect of the American military experience in this century cannot, however, be overlooked, and since some misunderstanding of the nature and requirements of armed forces may have deepened the impact of events in Vietnam, and since reference has already more than once been made to the reflection in armed service of the characteristics of parent societies, and what is now in mind offers a clear illustration of this, it is appropriate at this point to examine it.

Following pages: Helicopters land U.S. troops on Operation Eagle's Claw, South Vietnam, 14 February 1966

The American Civil War of 1861–5 was in many ways unique. It was the
first railway war, it was the first war of the electric telegraph, it was the first
war fought with canned rations, it was the first war to demonstrate the
ferocious effect of massed small arms fire, even before it became automatic.
It had many other aspects deserving close attention from military
professionals and it was not for nothing that for many years, and
particularly in my own generation, the American Civil War was a prime
object of study at the British Staff College. Most students there in that
generation knew rather more about Stonewall Jackson than they did about
the great Duke of Marlborough.

The Civil War left many deep imprints on the pattern of military
practice in the United States, one important one being the significance in
armies of territorial and regimental loyalties. This had possibly dwindled
(though the evidence suggests it had not disappeared) by the end of the
century. The U.S. Army was then in a state of some uncertainty and flux
when the outcome of the Spanish-American war landed the United States,
at the very turn of the century, with the hitherto unheard of responsibility
of the garrisoning and management of colonial territories overseas.
Evidence of error, incompetence and structural inadequacies in the conduct
of the war demanded radical change. In August 1899 President McKinley

brought in an able lawyer with no military experience, Elihu Root, as Secretary of War. Under two Presidents, McKinley and Roosevelt, Root carried out a complete reorganization of the army, creating a general staff and carrying out many other thoroughgoing changes in a term of office of conspicuous administrative ability. He also set off a process which was widely believed at the turn of the 1980s to have gone too far and to stand in need of correction – the almost total subordination of military practice in the United States to the methods of business and industry.

It has frequently been emphasized in what has already been said that the pattern of a parent society is faithfully reflected in the military institutions to which it gives birth and that developments in the first are followed sooner or later by corresponding developments in the second. The latter tend to happen of their own accord but they must be carefully watched and when they are seen to be moving in a direction injurious to the military institution they must be restrained and kept under some degree of control.

In the United States the huge logistical effort which, towards the end of the First World War, had assembled, organized and moved (with heavy Allied assistance in ordnance and shipping) two million men and seven and a half million tons of supplies to Europe in less than nineteen months, was only made possible by a radical rationalization and centralization of control. When the war was over the post-war rundown saw a reversion to the traditional pattern of fragmented, diffused authority and decentralized responsibilities. The swing of the pendulum at higher levels in the U.S. Army between traditionalists and rationalists was brought to an abrupt end some twenty years later with General Marshall's reorganization of March 1942. From then on there was an enormous increase in the application to defence of those business and industrial techniques in which the United States leads the world. The end of the Second World War might have seen another return of traditional patterns of organization. The Cold War and the persistent growth of Soviet military power prevented that. The revolution in technology and the steeply mounting costs of weapon systems demanded centralized control in research and development and in procurement. Management began to move in and to establish itself more and more, first of all as a support and then even as a substitute for leadership.

In operations of war, to whose successful conduct all military activity is directed, management and leadership are both indispensable. They are not the same thing. Some part of the functional area covered by each is common to both. The two areas are far from being coterminous. Put simply – too simply, perhaps, but conveniently – management chiefly concerns itself with knowing what to do; leadership with getting it done. Military activity demands both, in a mixture whose composition varies with the circumstances. It would seem that the higher the level of command and the greater the distance from what is sometimes called the 'sharp end', the higher the requirement for management; the lower the level and the closer the battle, the higher the need for leadership. Given that technical competence is a requirement everywhere, and assuming for our purpose its general adequacy, the good platoon commander must be a

continued on page 193

Cadets, U.S. Military Academy, West Point, 1902–1907

American Civil War, Battle of Corinth, 3–4 October 1862. Federal troops under General William Rosecrans successfully defend Corinth, thus ending the Confederate advance in the west (From a Kurtz and Allison lithograph)

Above: German machine-gun crew in action during the Second World War.

Right: 'Fall ich am Donaustrand? Sterb' ich in Polen?' *(Hugo Zuckermann, 1914). German wartime cemetery, First World War*

Left: First World War. A German U-boat sinks an armed free-running merchantman in a surface action

*U.S. Marines of the Second World War: poster for
a documentary film*

*Left: United States recruiting poster, First World
War (By James Montgomery Flagg: West Point
Museum)*

U.S. soldier armed with an Armalite assault rifle, c.1968

Left: Robert McNamara, U.S. Defense Secretary

Below: Elihu Root, U.S Secretary for War from August 1899, under Presidents McKinley and Roosevelt, to February 1904; a corporation lawyer whose influence on the management of defence in the U.S. has been profound

continued from page 184

competent manager in a limited sphere but the demands upon his powers of leadership can be very great. For an army commander the distribution of emphasis between management and leadership will be different. For the commander of a base installation even more markedly so.

The danger in the U.S. Army lay not in the assertion of the importance of management in relation to leadership but in what almost seemed an attempt to put management in leadership's place. The Second World War saw a big jump in the application of business techniques to military problems. It must be accepted that, given the American temperament and outlook and the huge success of the national approach to industry, this was largely inevitable. Tighter central controls, with greater functionalization and more rationalization, were features of the fifties, in which the use of outside management consultancy agencies and special commissions set up by Congress were prominent features. The managerial revolution in the U.S. armed forces, the culmination of the process set under way by Root, was completed under Defense Secretary McNamara, brought in from the Ford motor company. McNamara originated no new trends. He only strengthened earlier ones. Nevertheless the changes he introduced, particularly in the package he personally forced through on what some officers have called Black Friday, 8 December 1961, established the supremacy of Big Business methods in army management.

Some of the results deserve comment. Soldiers came more and more to be treated as impersonal items in an inventory, posted about as individuals to fill slots shown up on the computer. The effect on unit coherence, particularly overseas, was little short of disastrous. The fighting group has to be composed of men who know and trust each other. This becomes impossible when men are freely rotated in a system of single postings, or drafted in to strengthen, for some particular exercise, a unit which will never see them again. The effect of industrial management techniques on the officer corps was also bad, and even more injurious to unit coherence. Careers often came to be seen as more important than the units in which they were developed. Short tours of duty to demonstrate on an officer's personal records as wide as possible a variety of experience were more and more seen as aids to professional advancement. Units almost ceased to be coherent fighting groups, capable of serious joint resistance to combat stress. Companies, battalions, regiments were beginning to lose sight of themselves as recognizable entities.

As the seventies gave way to the eighties the restlessness of high and deeply dedicated professional officers in the U.S. Army, of which there are happily always many, began to make itself felt. The leadership and vision of an outstanding Chief of Staff began to seek changes, and first of all in strengthening the cohesion of the unit.

In my own service as a young officer any officer who stayed much less than two years in command of a squadron or company was regarded as little more than a transient. Times have changed. It is a measure of the change that the U.S. Army has now extended tours of company commanders to eighteen months. They have been as low as six to eight before. Unit identifications in dress and accoutrements are also being encouraged. Individual replacement is being reduced. The aim is soon to begin, as an innovation, rotating companies overseas. To British ears this is startling. The British Army has long been accustomed to rotating troops on overseas service, as a general rule, by battalions. Different armies have different characteristics and attract different criticisms. Whatever critics may say of the British Army, its standard of unit cohesion, based on the regimental system, is very high.

The U.S. Army is now cultivating once more its own version of the regimental system. There is in this, as in other respects, a wind of change blowing. The U.S. Army is moving once more towards a position where its parent society can relate to it with solid satisfaction and of which it can be proud. Everyone who values the freedoms of an open society should wish this movement well.[101]

Where does the 'gentleman' stand in the officer establishment today? There is no time to pursue this far. A view set out in the U.S.A. in 1950 in an official publication seems reasonable: 'The military officer is considered a gentleman . . . because nothing less . . . is truly suited for his particular set of responsibilities.'[102]

In relations between young officers and men, when consistency, firmness and sincerity are important and warmth of personal feelings must be tempered with some degree of detachment, the implications of what is said here are just. They are above all important where disciplinary questions arise, as happens inevitably under the terms of the military contract. These make heavy demands on the young officer, who has to be made to remember that only a person of liberal mind is entitled to exercise coercion over others in a society of free men.

It is worth remarking here that as an officer rises higher in his profession the demands made upon him in the administration of justice increase. The machine is efficient but must be most jealously watched. A senior officer who confirms punishments often has the power to modify or lessen them. He will not do so without most careful inquiry, to which he will also bring compassion and common sense. This can tax a whole mind and it brings its own rewards.

Whatever may be thought now about 'officers' and 'gentlemen', a change of critical importance in our time is in the rejection of the assumption that the qualities required of an officer are to be found only in one stratum of society. Criteria of social standing in deciding a man's suitability for officership, which have been applied for close on 2,000 years in Western society, with only rare and short-lived challenge, are now being modified.[103]

A patrol of the 1st Battalion The Coldstream Guards with their 'Ferret' armoured scout car on the border separating West Berlin from East Germany

The vestiges of the eighteenth-century distinction between gentle and simple, as reflected in relationships between officers and non-officers, are vanishing. An article in a popular weekly paper once pointed out that the disappearance of what it called the old feudal relationship, 'typical of the pre-war professional', is not without disadvantages. 'Many officers today,' said this newspaper, 'are nine-to-five types.'[104] The problem is to retain group coherences and a rational pattern of discipline and command without relying on moribund features in the social structure. This is a problem which the British Army, as that paper pointed out with considerable penetration, is trying to solve. It is a problem which in other national armies, American, French, Federal German, Soviet Russian, exists either in a form very different from that found in class-divided Britain or scarcely at all.

The distinction between officer and N.C.O. in any army of a major power is unlikely to disappear. There is, nonetheless, much to be said for a re-examination of the pattern of distribution of responsibilities between officers and N.C.O.s. It probably still takes too little account of the results of rising standards in living, education and general information amongst people almost everywhere in the Western world. The better and maturer minds required among officers in armed service today, moreover, will not be so readily attracted to it if the demands made upon the junior officer are too low. A consequent tendency has been evident to increase the responsibilities of the N.C.O. and to liberate the junior officer from some of the duties which make insufficient demands on the mental qualities expected in him. This tendency is likely to continue. If it results in further significant adjustment of areas of responsibility it could bring about a modification of the numerical relationship of officers to non-commissioned officers as well as in patterns of promotion and discipline.

On the officer side an interesting distinction is emerging in Western armies between those who are likely to become competitors for the higher posts and those who are not. A double career structure is being set up in different ways in different countries to take account of it.[105]

A distinction is worth pointing out here between professional education in the profession of arms and that in some other professions such as medicine or the law. In these emphasis is placed on a single long and concentrated dose, after which the practitioner, though he has very much still to learn, is recognized as qualified. In armies and to a lesser degree in navies and air forces the initial professional education dose is only enough for the earliest stages. Thereafter the officer who gets on in the service frequently goes back to school. In specialist courses in staff and command schools, and in advanced courses, he spends in armies where technical and professional standards are high (as in the U.S., the Federal Republic of Germany and in Britain) not less than one-fifth of his professional life on studies intended to prepare him for an extension of his experience or for greater responsibilities. This is vastly greater than the amount of time spent in this way in the law and rather more than in medicine.

The pattern of professional education in the armed services is progressive. There is consequently no intolerable waste of preparatory effort in the

policy now being widely applied in the armies of Western countries, under which those who are unlikely to rise high in their profession or are unwilling to stay in it long may leave early in order to re-establish themselves elsewhere while they are still young enough to do so. It is hoped to make their sojourn in the service attractive, enjoyable and fulfilling, for as long as it lasts, and to bring them out of it not less well placed to start somewhere else than if they had never joined.

In the U.S. and Britain, as in other countries, officer qualities are now sought in a deeper section of society than they were. Educational standards at entry and at various stages thereafter have been in general rising, even though recruiting problems have sometimes slowed down the rate of rise. Command by domination has long given way in significant degree to command by consent. Professionalism is more respected. In an army, the least technical (in a non-military sense) of the three or four main services into which national armed forces are commonly articulated, the requirements for technical awareness in ambitious officers have risen steeply in the last few years and are still rising. Speaking generally of service in the armies of the Western world, material rewards are not unsatisfactory during an officer's service and although pillage now plays no part in his expectations he can look forward to a pension when he retires which compares very favourably with what he could put by in other professions. Career prospects in terms of promotions are on the whole rational and, though there have been problems in some countries and reference has already been made to these, the criteria for advancement are generally sensible.

Improvements such as these have long been urgently required. I hope, and believe, they have been made in time. Others must follow. The social results of inadequacy in the management of violence in two world wars have already been enormous and remain incalculable. Since war became total we have acquired weapons which in total war can destroy mankind. The penalty of inadequacy was high before. It could now be final.

We struggle to escape from this situation. Opinion tends to move between two absolutist extremes. At one end are those who are convinced that total war must come; that it should be prepared for as a matter of the highest priority; that a favourable opportunity for it should be welcomed and even sought. Such unlikely companions as the pure Marxist-Leninist and the champion of unrestricted Capitalist free enterprise (both rather old-fashioned types) can easily find themselves together here. At the other extreme are all those who see no hope for mankind except in the rejection and suppression of all means of war, starting with the most destructive and making a brave and desperate gesture of voluntary surrender, if need be, in the hope that others will follow.

Somewhere between these two positions you will find most of the more intelligent professional officers. They are more pessimist than optimist in that they see little cause to suppose that man has morally so far advanced as to be able to refrain from violence. They tend to be more pragmatist than absolutist in that they reject the inevitability of total war at one end as totally intolerable, while they regard the notions of the total disarmers at the other as scarcely practicable. They do not, in sum, see why man, in spite

Sir John Hackett in his library at Coberley Mill in 1983

199

of his ineradicable tendency to violence, should be unable to manage the affairs of the world without blowing it up, even though he now knows how to do it and cannot be forced to forget; but they realize that the solution of these problems demands more good minds in the profession of arms than have been found there in the past.

The regularization of the profession was accompanied by a marked rise in the threshold between the military and civilian areas of activity. Barrack life, uniforms, increased specialization in military skills, the growth in extent and complexity of formal military administration were among the factors contributing to set the soldier more apart from the civilian. The distinction between the specialist in warfare on land and at sea also grew more marked.

As the profession grew more professional, first at sea and then on land, the sailor and the soldier moved further apart from each other and the functional area in which both operated, the military, grew ever more sharply distinct from the non-military. The development of aerial warfare in the early twentieth century led to the specialization of a third type of armed service whose relation to the other two has varied from time to time and country to country and whose future locus and function are at present obscure. All that can be said is that they are likely to be largely determined by technical developments.

As professionalization proceeded, the professional was allowed more of a prescriptive right to authoritative judgment in his own sphere. Not unnaturally this was most noticeable where the rate of advance in professionalism was highest, that is, in nineteenth-century Germany. Here the success of the military in ordering their own affairs and the obvious

Sergeant of the 12th U.S. Marine Regiment receives the Silver Star from his C.O. in Vietnam, February 1967

Germany, 1956: Major General Hackett inspects the 13th/18th Hussars

national advantages which resulted led to a widespread belief in a capacity in the military for successful organization in non-military areas. They claimed the expertness of the initiate and were accorded as well a discretionary right of judgment in other spheres than their own. In mid-twentieth-century Germany the area of activity within which the military establishment is encouraged to operate has been sharply curtailed. Conversely, in other states of which all too many instances will come to mind, the effectiveness of the military in maintaining an orderly structure when civil political constitutions prove too frail to do so has resulted in assumption by the military of civil functions. Praetorianism is widespread; its growth must be watched with deep misgiving.

It is worth saying here that the degree of recognition of what might be called purely military factors seems to vary roughly as the degree of freedom of the military from civilian control. It remained high in Germany until the Second World War. It was higher in France in 1912 than it is now seventy years later. It is higher now in the United States than it was in 1912. It has never been high in Britain.

The movement of the military away from the civil has now in general been reversed. They have come closer together. Military skills are less exclusively specialist. The military community lives less apart. Uniforms are less worn in civilian society. The working clothes of a general in the field are very like those of a machine-minder, though he still has something rather more grand put by for special occasions. All soldiers like to put on pretty clothes now and then, just as academics do.

How far will this tendency to reintegration go? Not, I am sure, as far as a complete merger. The special nature of the military calling will persist, and though the threshold between civil and military has in recent years got lower, and may get lower still, it is unlikely in my opinion to disappear. It is the task of those in charge to determine its optimum height, or, to put it another way, to see how close the military can be brought to the civilian without destroying the value of the soldier to society. One thing is recognized as particularly important: to minimize the difficulty of reintegration when the soldier wishes to cross the threshold and become a civilian.

I have mentioned this before and do so again only to emphasize its importance, which has risen sharply in the last two decades. Probably in no country has the requirement yet been fully met, but in every one the effort is being made. A civilian qualification for every military professional, or at least skills saleable in civil life, is the ideal. In Britain, which is where I know educational problems best, particularly where service education is concerned, more than 300 young officers out of a small army are currently reading for university degrees in the army's time, on the army's payroll, and the other services are certainly doing in other ways no less. Meanwhile, a sizeable cohort of middle-rank officers is doing postgraduate work and I rejoice whenever I find it being done, as is readily permitted, in what might be called non-military topics – mediaeval manuscripts, for instance, or classical epigraphy.

How then does the military calling look to one who has followed it for half man's allotted span of three score years and ten and sees absolutely no reason for regret that he has done so? It is one of the fundamental pursuits. There are occupations in which what is demanded of those who pursue them cannot be entirely regulated by contracts between men. The compulsions exerted in these occupations arise mainly from the nature of the task itself. They include those of the priest, the healer, the lawgiver, the craftsman, the teacher, the scholar, the seaman and the farmer. These are not merely mechanical pursuits.[106] Among them the profession of arms deserves (and I believe it has) a respected place.

The essential basis of the military life is the ordered application of force under an unlimited liability. It is the unlimited liability which sets the man who embraces this life somewhat apart. He will be (or should be) always a citizen. So long as he serves he will never be a civilian.

There are many ways of looking at a soldier. He can be regarded as no more than a military mechanic: a military operation can be considered as just another engineering project. This is a mistake which I have already discussed. It can lead to unfortunate results when the unlimited liability clause in the unwritten contract is invoked as the operation unfolds.

He can be regarded, rather emotionally and too simply, as a hired assassin. Only those who do not know many soldiers can maintain this view with confidence. If soldiers were only paid killers their calling would have done something to them which you can look for in vain.

The soldier can be thought of as one of de Vigny's great shaggy dogs of grenadiers, mournful, sweet-tempered and doomed.

British officers of the Transjordan Frontier Force on the steps of the Cavalry Club, London, setting out for Buckingham Palace to receive gallantry awards for active service in Palestine, 1939. Captain Hackett is on the right

Germany 1956: the G.O.C. of 7th Armoured Division at a Christmas party

The soldier has been romanticized, reviled, esteemed, derided. He has been the target of some of the best invective, Voltaire's[107] for example or Shaw's. I particularly recommend the preface of *John Bull's Other Island (Down With the Soldier)* as sane and refreshing reading for every regular officer. To see how far Shaw is wrong today is as important as to see how far he is still right, and to make sure we continue to steer the profession of arms away from his own picture of it. Shaw is as angry as Voltaire and for the same reason: man obstinately remains what he is and declines to become what the radical reformer thinks he ought to be. The very existence of the profession of arms is a constant reminder that this is so and the rancour it sometimes arouses in the radical breast is easily understood.

George Bernard Shaw wrote the play John Bull's Other Island, *a penetrating analysis of Anglo–Irish relations and a brilliant plea for Home Rule, in 1904. He published a preface to it in 1906. Britain was then at the apogee of Empire. Much has happened since: colonial rule in the old imperial style has all but vanished and the military means by which it was sustained, so savagely attacked here in ferocious caricature by G.B.S., have vanished with it. Shaw was often carried by the strength of his enthusiasms and his delight in the handling of language to a degree of exaggeration which was probably intended and was certainly valuable. It irritated the reader out of complacency and made him look more carefully at what he had formerly taken too much for granted. That is why the passage in the preface to* John Bull's Other Island *headed 'Down With the Soldier' should probably be read by every regular officer and why it is reproduced here.*

. . . The soldier is an anachronism of which we must get rid. Among people who are proof against the suggestions of romantic fiction there can no longer be any question of the fact that military service produces moral imbecility, ferocity, and cowardice, and that the defence of nations must be undertaken by the civil enterprise of men enjoying all the rights and liberties of citizenship, and trained by the exacting discipline of democratic freedom and responsibility. For permanent work the soldier is worse than useless: such efficiency as he has is the result of dehumanization and disablement. His whole training tends to make him a weakling. He has the easiest of lives: he has no freedom and no responsibility. He is politically and socially a child, with rations instead of rights, treated like a child, punished like a child, dressed prettily and washed and combed like a child, excused for outbreaks of naughtiness like a child, forbidden to marry like a child, and called Tommy like a child. He has no real work to keep him from going mad except housemaid's work: all the rest is forced exercise, in the form of endless rehearsals for a destructive and terrifying performance which may never come off, and which, when it does come off, is not like the rehearsals. His officer has not even housekeeper's work to keep him sane. The work of organizing and commanding bodies of men, which builds up the character and resource of the large class of civilians who live by it, only demoralizes the military officer, because his orders, however disastrous or

Sir John Hackett at home, 1983. 'The Good Shepherd . . . Alas! What boots it with uncessant care to tend the homely, slighted, shepherds' trade? And strictly meditate the thankless Muse? Were it not better done, as others use, to sport with Amaryllis in the shade . . .?' (John Milton, Lycidas I, 64)

offensive, must be obeyed without regard to consequences: for instance, if he calls his men dogs, and perverts a musketry drill order to make them kneel to him as an act of personal humiliation, and thereby provokes a mutiny among men not yet thoroughly broken in to the abjectness of the military condition, he is not, as might be expected, shot, but, at worst, reprimanded, whilst the leader of the mutiny, instead of getting the Victoria Cross and a public testimonial, is condemned to five years' penal servitude by Lynch Law (technically called martial law) administered by a trade union of officers. Compare with this the position of, for instance, our railway managers or our heads of explosive factories. They have to handle large bodies of men whose carelessness or insubordination may cause wholesale destruction of life and property; yet any of these men may insult them, defy them, or assault them without special penalties of any sort. The military commander dares not face these conditions: he lives in perpetual terror of his men, and will undertake their command only when they are stripped of all their civil rights, gagged, and bound hand and foot by a barbarous slave code. Thus the officer learns to punish, but never to rule; and when an emergency [. . .] comes, he breaks down; and the situation has to be saved by a few untypical officers with character enough to have retained their civilian qualities in spite of the messroom . . .

. . . we have had . . . sensational demonstrations of the fact that soldiers pay the penalty of their slavery and outlawry by becoming, relatively to free civilians, destructive, cruel, dishonest, tyrannical, hysterical, mendacious, alarmists at home and terrorists abroad, politically reactionary, and professionally incapable. If it were humanly possible to militarize all the humanity out of a man, there would be absolutely no defence to this indictment. But the military system is so idiotically academic and impossible, and renders its victims so incapable of carrying it out with any thoroughness except when, in an occasional hysterical outburst of terror and violence, that hackneyed comedy of civil life, the weak man putting his foot down, becomes the military tragedy of the armed man burning, flogging, and murdering in a panic, that a body of soldiers and officers is in the main, and under normal circumstances, much like any other body of laborers and gentlemen. Many of us count among our personal friends and relatives officers whose amiable and honorable character seems to contradict everything I have just said about the military character. You have only to describe Lynch courts and acts of terrorism to them as the work of Ribbonmen, Dacoits, Moonlighters, Boxers, or – to use the general term most familiar to them – 'natives', and their honest and generous indignation knows no bounds: they feel about them like men, not like soldiers. But the moment you bring the professional side of them uppermost by describing precisely the same proceedings to them as the work of regular armies, they defend them, applaud them, and are ready to take part in them as if their humanity had been blown out like a candle. You find that there is a blind spot on their moral retina, and that this blind spot is the military spot.

The excuse, when any excuse is made, is that discipline is supremely important in war. Now most soldiers have no experience of war; and to assume that those who have are therefore qualified to legislate for it, is as absurd as to assume that a man who has been run over by an omnibus is thereby qualified to draw up wise regulations for the traffic of London. Neither our military novices nor our veterans are clever enough to see that in the field, discipline either keeps itself or goes to pieces; for humanity under fire is a quite different thing from humanity in barracks: when there is danger the difficulty is never to find men who will obey, but men who can command. It is in time of peace, when an army is either a police force (in which case its work can be better done by a civilian constabulary) or an absurdity, that discipline is difficult, because the wasted life of the soldier is unnatural, except to a lazy man, and his servitude galling and senseless, except to a docile one. Still, the soldier is a man, and the officer sometimes a gentleman in the literal sense of the word; and so, what with humanity, laziness, and docility combined, they manage to rub along with only occasional outbursts of mutiny on the one side and class rancour and class cowardice on the other.

They are not even discontented; for the military and naval codes simplify life for them just as it is simplified for children. No soldier is asked to think for himself, to judge for himself, to consult his own honor and manhood, to dread any consequence except the consequence of punishment to his own person. The rules are plain and simple; the ceremonies of respect and submission are as easy and mechanical as a prayer wheel; the orders are always to be obeyed thoughtlessly, however inept or dishonorable they may be. As the late Laureate said in the two stinging lines in which he branded the British soldier with the dishonor of Esau, 'theirs not to reason why, theirs but to do and die'. To the moral imbecile and political sluggard these conditions are as congenial and attractive as they are abhorrent and intolerable to the William Tell temperament. Just as the most incorrigible criminal is always, we are told, the best behaved convict, so the man with least conscience and initiative makes the best behaved soldier, and that not wholly through mere fear of punishment, but through a genuine fitness for and consequent happiness in the childlike military life. Such men dread freedom and responsibility as a weak man dreads a risk or a heavy burden; and the objection to the military system is that it tends to produce such men by a weakening disuse of the moral muscles. No doubt this weakness is just what the military system aims at, its ideal soldier being, not a complete man, but a docile unit of cannonfodder which can be trusted to respond promptly and certainly to the external stimulus of a shouted order, and is intimidated to the pitch of being afraid to run away from a battle. It may be doubted whether even in the Prussian heyday of the system, when floggings of hundreds and even thousands of lashes were matters of ordinary routine, this detestable ideal was ever realized; but your courts-martial are not practical enough to take that into account: it is characteristic of the military mind continually to ignore human nature and cry for the moon instead of facing modern social facts and accepting modern democratic conditions. And when I say the military mind, I repeat that I am not forgetting the patent fact that the military mind and the humane mind can exist in the same person; so that an officer who will take all the civilian risks, from city traffic to fox-hunting, without uneasiness, and who will manage all the civil employees on his estate and in his house and stables without the aid of a Mutiny Act, will also, in his military capacity, frantically declare that he dare not walk about in a foreign country unless every crime of violence against an Englishman in uniform is punished by the bombardment and destruction of a whole village, or the wholesale flogging and execution of every native in the neighborhood, and also that unless he and his fellow officers have power, without the intervention of a jury, to punish the slightest self-assertion or hesitation to obey orders, however grossly insulting or disastrous those orders may be, with sentences which are reserved in civil life for the worst crimes, he cannot secure the obedience and respect of his men, and the country will accordingly lose all its colonies and dependencies, and be helplessly conquered in the German invasion which he confidently expects to occur in the course of a fortnight or so. That is to say, in so far as he is an ordinary gentleman he behaves sensibly and courageously; and in so far as he is a military man he gives way without shame to the grossest folly, cruelty, and poltroonery. If any other profession in the world had been stained by these vices, and by false witness, forgery, swindling, torture, compulsion of men's families to attend their executions, digging up and mutilation of dead enemies, all wantonly added to the devastation proper to its own business, as the military profession has been within recent memory in England, France, and the United States of America (to mention no other countries), it would be very difficult to induce men of capacity and character to enter it. And in England it is, in fact, largely dependent for its recruits on the refuse of industrial life, and for its officers on the aristocratic and plutocratic refuse of political and diplomatic life, who join the army and pay for their positions in the more or less fashionable clubs which the regimental messes provide them with – clubs which, by the way, occasionally figure in ragging scandals as circles of extremely coarse moral character.

Now in countries . . . in which the government does not rest on the consent of the people, it must rest on military coercion; and the bureaucracy, however civil and legal it may be in form and even in the character of its best officials, must connive at all the atrocities of military rule, and become infected in the end with the chronic panic characteristic of militarism . . .

The man-at-arms is different things at different times to the same people. 'Our God and soldiers we alike adore/ev'n at the brink of danger; not before.'[108] He can be looked at in a thousand different ways, for he is an inevitable phenomenon in human society. More poetry has been written about him and his doings, about fighting men and warfare, than about anything else on earth, not excluding the love of men for women.

In his professional environment he lives an ordered life. It is the sort of life which Cicero admired, lived *ordine et modo*.[109] Its orderliness is liberating rather than oppressive. It is far from incompatible with Christianity. The record of the actions of Jesus Christ in the Gospels show him forbearing to soldiers, even kind. He was rough with politicians, lawyers, financiers, professors and divines.

There is satisfaction in service, there is satisfaction in an ordered life, there is satisfaction in the progressive mastery of complex skills, and there is satisfaction in professional association with men of a high average level of integrity. But the service has to be service to what is worthwhile, and the ordered life has to lead somewhere. The professional skills must be

A guardsman on the assault course, during initial training at Pirbright, 1953

209

interesting and around them must be a wide area of choice in other pursuits. It is upon these points that the young man considering armed service must satisfy himself. I do not think he will be disappointed.

The primary function of an armed force is to fight in battle. This is nowadays impossible without a highly complex system of supporting activities. Among these a man may find not only the chance of self-fulfilment in a closely coherent group of human beings, where confidence is generally high and everyone receives from others what he is prepared to give. He will also be offered an opportunity for pretty nearly every pursuit that appeals to the rational man.

I only ever knew one general in my own service who had one of his paintings hung in the British Royal Academy. We had read classics together in the same college at Oxford, he a year or two my senior, and then joined different Irish cavalry regiments in the British services – with horses: thank God we were in time for that. I was later to take over from him as Deputy Chief of Staff in London. This man's achievement in the arts was unusual but there are many generals who paint and do it well. Probably not many are masters of the language in Russian, Arabic or classical Cantonese, but almost any young officer in most Western armies able and willing to study a language for two or three years will be encouraged to do so and probably spend some of this time abroad at his employer's expense. If he is of unusual capacity as a scientist he might find himself, after a first degree at a university, again at his employer's expense, reading for a doctorate or at least a master's degree. The young officer can paint, sail boats, play a musical instrument, join an expedition, learn mathematics, go mountaineering – help himself in short to a variety of pursuits active or reflective, not as things he has to struggle to do but as things which the system in which he has made his life encourages and sometimes even helps to pay for.

Make no mistake about it: the military establishment is not a philanthropic body. It has good reason to encourage these things. First, there are skills (and a very wide range of them) whose availability in armed forces is deemed important. Secondly, there are activities which develop the mental, moral and physical qualities required in the efficient fighting man. Thirdly, the life must be attractive to the right young men if the function of armed forces is to be efficiently discharged. The things I speak of as examples fall under one or more of these heads, most under all three.

Some men are dissatisfied if they become too separated from the earth upon which they live, and what happens on and round it. I realized myself as a young officer that I should not have been content doing anything for a living in which it was never important to me what time the sun rose. Dawn, dusk, moonrise and moonset, what the wind does, the shape and size of woodland, marsh and hill, currents and tides, the flow of rivers and the form of clouds, whether the leaf is on the tree or the branches are bare, the seasons, the weather and the stars – these are matters of compelling importance in the lives of sailors, soldiers, airmen, some of more importance to one, some to another. So, too, at all times and above all, are people.

In measuring the worth of any way of life a study of its average products will not tell you what you want to know. Those who display its essential characteristics in exceptional degree are more informative, a Colonel Newcome, let us say, or a Jos Sedley. Perhaps even more misleading than to regard the average is to look only at the worst. To see how bad men can be in any profession is to learn little about it worth knowing. Ask instead what opportunities it gives to those the ancient Greeks called μεγάθυμοι, the men of great soul.

The profession of arms is an essential social institution offering an orderly way of life, set a little apart, not without elegance. 'The performance of public duty is not the whole of what makes a good life,' said Bertrand Russell, in language that would have pleased Cicero; 'there is also the pursuit of private excellence.'[110] Both are to be found in the military life. It gives much and takes more, enriching freely anyone prepared to give more than he gets. It will remain with us for as long as man continues to be what he is, too clever and not good enough. This looks like being a long time yet.

Leadership

It is said that there was once a young platoon officer who was believed by his commanding officer to be inclined to run away in battles. This belief was shared by the men in the platoon, not without reason. But the men liked this young officer and wished him no harm. They therefore backed him up stoutly on the battlefield so that he should feel less inclined to run away.

The commanding officer was uneasy about this platoon commander and as soon as possible replaced him with another young officer about whose braveness there was no possible question. When the platoon went into action the new platoon commander was as brave as expected. But now the men ran away.

That little piece of folklore is ill authenticated and probably misleading. At best it contains no more than a fragmentary statement. But it does two things. First, it indicates the very complex nature of this problem and so will help me, I hope, to excuse myself from offering a coherent and systematic analysis of it. Secondly, it suggests the truth of what that wise old soldier the Maréchal de Saxe used to say. There is nothing more important in war than the human heart. 'In a knowledge of the human heart,' says the Marshal, 'must be sought the secrets of the success and failure of armies.' Our knowledge of the heart, he added, was very imperfect. Would he find it any less so today, I wonder?

But anyone who tries to get other people to do things, in whatever sphere, is faced by problems of which many are essentially similar.

The environment of battle, where pressures are high, causes problems of leadership to stand out in bold relief and that is, perhaps, why some of these problems are worth looking at in a military context.

It is worth remembering from the start that military practice is group practice. The military art is deeply concerned with the performance of the human group under stress.

Let me also remark here that in spite of the absence in military service in peace of some of the deeper stresses found in war, the management of a major military group, that is, command of a unit, is in many respects more difficult in peacetime than it is in war. In wartime, for example, there are few financial constraints. The functional efficiency of your equipment is what matters most then and you are not so closely pressed to account for it. In peacetime you have duties connected with the affairs of soldiers' families, with welfare, with education, with barrack maintenance, with public occasions, with competitive sports, with a variety of inspections and with many other things which leave you untroubled on active service. In war you only have to be brave, competent, tireless and calm – but not all the time. This is far easier than what is required of you in peace. Besides, the company is particularly good in war, above all at the sharp end, to which the logical man who gets mixed up in a war will surely find his way.

For the discharge of the function of leadership, the establishment of a dominant position for the leader over the led is indispensable. How does this come about?

In the archetypal leader/follower relationship it seems to happen of its own accord. I do not mean here the establishment of dominance by brute force and fear. In all I have to say here I am concerned pretty well exclusively with subordination by consent.

The leader has something which the others want and which only he can provide. The man who can show the tribesmen where the water-hole is has a special knowledge: he can direct those in need to the place where their need can be satisfied. But you would call him no more than a guide and not a leader unless something else were present. This something is partly the ability to find an answer to a problem which the others cannot solve. But there is also the power, when difficulties have to be overcome, to help people over them. A capacity to help people in the overcoming of the difficulties which face them in a joint enterprise is one of those things which distinguish the person who is a leader from the person who is no more than a guide.

In the more complex leader/follower relationship which you find in a modern army the leader is still giving something which the led require. All are bound together in a common undertaking whose success is of common concern. In the basic military environment – not that of most frequent occurrence, but the basic situation – that is, in battle, success in the common enterprise is usually of the very highest importance to nearly everyone concerned. The higher the morale of the military entity, the closer its coherence, the more completely will success in the enterprise be desired. What the leader has to give is the direction of a joint effort which will bring success. That is what he is there for, and he must have sufficient mastery of the techniques involved to do what is demanded of him by those he leads. Very early on in the enquiry, you will notice, there emerges the suggestion that the function of leadership cannot be discharged on the one side without a requirement to be led on the other.

To make a commanding position over other men acceptable to them it is also necessary for the man holding it to possess in a higher degree than they do qualities which they respect. I am quite sure that expertness in some relevant professional skill is also indispensable here. I am talking now not of his specific skill as a manager but of their skills as subordinate agents.

You have in fact, as it seems to me, to be good at what is done by professionals under your management if you are to exercise effective leadership over them, especially where the leader/follower relationship comes under considerable strain. It is not good enough any longer to be able simply to co-ordinate, in military affairs any more than in industrial enterprises, and the heavier the stresses the more clearly this emerges.

I do not mean to imply that the leader must possess in dominant degree a mastery of all the skills practised by those subordinate to him, or even all the more important ones. In any army this is now impossible. I suppose the Maréchal de Saxe might have been one of the last commanders who was master of even most of the more important skills employed in his army.

But in my own submission the leader, besides being a competent manager, must be known to possess a high degree of competence in some specific skill or skills closely relevant to the discharge of his organization's primary task. Thus you would expect to find that a field commander enjoyed a considerable reputation as, say, an infantry soldier or an artilleryman, or an armoured commander, before he was acceptable at higher levels of command, at division, for example, or corps.

Of course people set in authority at all levels in an army can be carried along by the machine itself, caught up in its rank structure. But when this happens the relationship between leaders and led may be too weak to withstand strain. It is very likely to break down when stress is heavy – under the stress, for example, which is produced by fear.

Can we distinguish between the qualities required in any leadership situation and the qualities required in specific situations, between main qualities and ancillary? I believe there is such a distinction, but it is not easy to draw. Knowing what it is best to do is important but knowing how to get things done seems to me clearly more so. The need for vocational or, if you like, professional competence in the man in charge is pronounced, as I have suggested, but in a group under stress this, by itself, is unlikely to be enough.

In fact, the heavier the stress on a group the higher the importance of what I might call personal qualities as distinct from professional competence. The relationship between these two areas is very complex and in the structure of a hierarchic organization, such as a regular army, it must be approached with care. Selection of personnel, training methods, the system of appointment and promotion – all these are matters in which this relationship is closely concerned. They need the most careful handling and deep and sympathetic attention.

The essential leadership situation does not arise unless there is a recognized requirement by someone to be led. Leadership is, in fact, a response on one side to an awareness of need on the other.

It is just worthwhile, perhaps, pointing out here that the relationship between a leader and those led is essentially different in one important respect when looked at from different ends of the nexus. The leader leads a group. However much he seeks to bind the members together in it by individual treatment his responsibility is over the group and to them as a whole. The member of the group, on the other hand, however much he may be bound together with the other members, responds to the leader essentially as an individual.

There is a much debated point here upon which Tolstoy has a good deal to say in *War and Peace*. He argues that Napoleon was not cause but product: he emerged as a dominant figure in response to a need. Napoleon did not himself bring about the situation in which he became supreme, but when this situation had come about it posed a problem to which Napoleon was the most nearly approximate answer.

I have heard the same thought expressed about other significant leaders – about Hitler and about Churchill too. When the need for leadership arises, so the theory goes, the person to satisfy it emerges, though it may be that those requiring to be led have to try out and reject more than one possibility before they get what suits them.

Whether the person who emerges as leader is fully adequate to the demands made upon him is a matter of complete chance. He may be very good indeed at this particular thing, like Churchill. He may be less good. It would be untrue to say that the degree of need is the principal determinant of the quality of the leadership it calls into being. But there would appear to be little doubt that unless there is a requirement to be led the function of leadership cannot be discharged.

Often, when the requirement to be led urgently arises, a pattern of subordination has already been formalized and leaders and led already have labels on them. But the person who can then effectively furnish what is required, the person who in the event takes effective charge, may not be the one with the right label.

A notable illustration of this is given in the play by the whimsical British playwright J. M. Barrie, *The Admirable Crichton*, which deals with the adventures of an aristocratic British family cast away on a Pacific island. In Barrie's play the butler Crichton responded to a need arising among the castaways which had certainly not arisen in the country house environment at home. He was now, by force of character and competence, the leader. When the castaways were rescued and restored to their former environment and they were all at home again the old writing on the tickets once more became important and the man who was labelled 'butler' was again subordinate to the man who was labelled 'master' – and the butler's hand in marriage ceased to be quite so desirable for the daughter of the house.

Under the pressures of battle, which can be very high, the requirement to be led emerges strongly. The stresses of the situation prepare subordinates for the acceptance of the direction which then comes in response to their need. It is because the stresses are so high in battle that the essential factors of the general leadership situation are, as I suggested earlier, so conveniently studied in the environment of field soldiering.

The power of example is very important to people under stress. For one thing it affords an outlet for hero worship, to which there seems to be an important and deep-rooted inclination in men. The person under stress is aware of inadequacies. He sees someone else apparently less burdened in this way. To some extent he identifies with that other person. This gives him some release. He is then likely to be grateful and become even more biddable. He will be even more open to the influence of suggestion and example than he was before.

In a battle the example of officers is the keystone of morale. Lord Moran, in that wise and compassionate book *The Anatomy of Courage*, refers to 'the electrifying effect of an act of coolness and courage on the part of an officer'.

A great part of this effect is, I believe, due to a sudden surge of relief in those who are witnesses. They are helped to shed a part at least of the intolerable burden of inadequacy under which they labour. They see another man doing what they long to do and cannot, someone being what they long to be and are not. Hope and purpose are shown to them where they labour in futility and despair and a rush of gratitude and humility and love can be the result.

Effective leadership in battle, I have suggested, depends more on knowing how to get things done than on being good at knowing what it would be best to do. Nonetheless, a group of people can often be dominated by the one person who sees most clearly, and can best explain, the issue. Bewildered men turn, as children do to grown-ups, towards anyone who can help to clear the confusion in their minds. Even to create in confused men the illusion that their minds have been cleared can have a similar effect. When effectively done, the clarification of an issue can act upon people under pressure like a magnet.

I have sometimes tried to make this point to groups of young officers. It suggests, however unlikely this may appear to some of them, that the classroom and, even more, the library, can make a very important contribution to powers of leadership in battle.

Liddell Hart recalls the surprise with which he found that his commanding officer had reported on him that the men 'would follow Captain Hart to the very depths of hell'. The rather obvious soldierly cliché must be forgiven: the Colonel's prose style was not as limpid as that of the officer he was reporting on. Liddell Hart was surprised because, he says, 'I had never felt that I possessed the obvious characteristics and magnetism of leadership'. Neither he did, in my opinion, but he is right in going on to emphasize 'how readily men respond to any lead which shows a grasp of the problem and gives them the feeling that . . . they would not be used recklessly or stupidly'. He refers to this realization as a 'basic condition' in 'effective leadership'.

I have seen the same sort of thing happen the other way round. A subaltern of mine in the desert was a rugged likeable chap, consistent, firm and humorous. He had a great way with the men but he was too brave by a long chalk. Soldiers were sometimes reluctant to follow him because they were not confident that there was a good enough chance of coming out again. Later, in Korea, this officer had become much more cautious – his earlier self would have called him timid. He was then one of the very best squadron leaders in battle in the whole campaign.

Another point worth making, perhaps, is that the same man is not necessarily as effective at one level of command as at another. 'I have seen very good Colonels,' says the Maréchal de Saxe, 'make very bad generals.' And of that other Marshal, Montgomery, Liddell Hart says that, as a young officer, 'He did not show the natural *signs* of leadership, or a knack of handling men – indeed, when he was eventually given command of a battalion, after sixteen years on the staff,' so Liddell Hart says, 'he brought it to the verge of mutiny by misjudged handling.' This was in peace of course, when the job is harder. Liddell Hart goes on to describe Montgomery as an outstanding example of how 'born commanders' can be surpassed by a 'made commander'.

Of born or natural leaders there never seem to be enough. They will be too few for an army, that is, which seems to use about one officer to ten other ranks. There just do not appear to be enough men with a sufficient degree of betterness, in relation to their fellows in relevant modes, to throw up one recognized leader in eleven by natural selection.

Hence, there is in armies a tendency to set up an officer group with an otherness as a step towards, or if necessary even in some degree a replacement of, the betterness you require. The officer is set apart, clothed differently and given distinguishing marks. His greater responsibilities are rewarded by greater privileges. There is some insistence on a show of respect. He is removed from that intimate contact with the men under his command which can throw such a strain upon the relationship of subordination. It is well known to old hands in the army that a lance corporal's job in maintaining discipline is harder than a subaltern's, for he has to live with the men.

Frederick the Great, in his *Instructions for the Generals*, says: 'A perfect general, like Plato's republic, is a figment of the imagination.' He goes on to refer to the necessity for dissimulation: he says that the general is 'constantly on the stage'.

When I was a cavalry subaltern my old troop sergeant, at a much lower level, used to say much the same. 'Remember, Sir,' he used to say, 'it is all a matter of bluff, Sir, really.'

The skills differ now. A requirement to excel in them remains. So does the requirement for a self-confident disregard of one's own inadequacies – which was probably what my Sergeant Leigh used to mean by 'bluff'.

In military leadership in the field, at low levels particularly, the man in charge has to be able to take more. He must have room for other people's troubles in addition to his own. This is not always easy, but the effort to contrive it has a most stimulating effect on the person making the effort. Officers who would probably break down in battle under the burden of their own troubles are often helped on by strength gained through a responsibility which causes them to take some of the load off others.

But perhaps the two most important things in the relation between a young officer and his men are consistency and sincerity. 'You know where you are with him' is high marks.

The treatment of failure by the man in charge in battle is a critical matter. This is a study on its own. A man caught on the rebound from failure can be a wonderful investment. When I was a squadron leader in the desert two men, a tank driver and a tank gunner who were pretty thick together, were largely responsible, in an obscure and probably discreditable way, for the death of the officer in their tank. To me, as the squadron leader, there seemed to be only two courses open. The obvious course was to get rid of them at once, to send them out of the battle in disgrace. On reflection I decided to take the other course instead. There was only one other. This was to make them the driver and gunner in my own tank. I did this and in all the fighting we had together thereafter they were splendid. I have rarely known a higher degree of confidence in a tank crew.

This was not taking much of a risk. It was very nearly a stone cold certainty. An opportunity to re-establish himself in his own esteem, when he has forfeited it, is something for which a man will give you a great deal in return.

I have had this opportunity given to me too: I know what it is like from the other end. There are not many benefits for which the recipient feels bound to offer something in return, but this is one, and the return is often a bountiful one.

Just as to help in the restoration of a man's self-respect – or to give him a chance to retrieve it – earns you a bountiful reward, so care is necessary not to impair this self-respect in, for example, reprimand.

'This is unlike you' can be far more effective and much less damaging to your relationship than 'There you go again, you useless so-and-so'.

But here again the man must know that you want to help. It is really less what you say than the assessment of your motive in saying it that matters. I have heard the most frightful things said to men by officers who lost nothing whatsoever of men's respect and liking in saying them because the intention was helpful and clear and there was no misunderstanding. The men knew the officer sought nothing for himself, in self-esteem, or build-up, or release. We have all seen, too, how people can treat their subordinates with impeccable politeness and receive nothing in return but disdain. 'Many secretly seek themselves in what they do,' I read in Thomas à Kempis, 'and know it not.'

I want to ask you to allow me, now, to say something about a capability which, in the fighting man, can probably with justice be described as a professional skill: it is not uniquely demanded in the military profession, but it has high importance there and it is the skill in which above all others the leader must be at least as proficient as the led and preferably more so. It is the management of fear.

Unless a commander possesses the respect of his subordinates in this particular regard the leader/follower relationship may prove too frail to withstand the strains of battle.

Everybody gets frightened. This is basic. I do not believe that many soldiers are frightened of death. Most people are frightened of dying and everybody is frightened of being hurt. The pressures of noise, of weariness, of insecurity lower the threshold of a man's resistance to fear. All these sources of stress can be found in battle, and others too – hunger, thirst, pain, excess of heat or cold and so on. Fear in war finds victims fattened for the sacrifice.

Men often get quite expert in managing themselves in relation to fear. Some also get quite good at managing others. Everyone knows how he has handled this problem himself and it is not easy to generalize. But it is perhaps true to say that one of the most effective ways of overcoming fear is what might be called the exclusion of the alternative.

A man suddenly faced with a terrifying situation – such as the appearance of a strong party of the enemy on patrol when he is a sentry in an outpost, alone, far from his friends and at night – may feel strongly inclined to run away. He will only do this if running away is a possible alternative to staying there. If this alternative does not exist for him, he not only will not run away: he cannot. The complete rejection of the possibility of any alternative course to the prescribed one is a great source of strength.

Honour, personal integrity – these are powerful aids in offering resistance to fear. An imaginative and sensitive man who has been unable entirely to exclude the option of flight will often not run away because to do so would tear his own personal integrity apart and inflict upon him wounds beside which the rending of his physical person would be more acceptable. He might be persuaded that he could not bear the thought of living as the sort of person the act of submission to fear would make of him, particularly where his act of submission has done very great harm to his friends.

But however fear is managed, unless a man knows at least as well how to manage it as those committed to his charge in battle his leadership is apt to falter. He must also be able to help others in the management of theirs.

The art (it is no less) of helping men to manage their fears can no more be imparted than that of the violinist or the painter, though some of the techniques can be studied. Sublimation in any form is important. Activity, hard physical work, can help. So can an opportunity for a defiant gesture. A padre I knew was a very brave man but he was always first into a slit trench when the enemy's fighter-bombers attacked us. This puzzled me, until he was discovered one day during such an attack lying on his back in the slit trench, safe – as he hoped – from detection, squirting away with a Bren gun. He said he knew he was doing wrong but it made him feel better.

If you can capture men's attention, and above all make them laugh, you are doing pretty well. Few medicines are as strong as this one. The release of laughter is one of the most valuable.

Some leaders at quite low levels get very good at all this, but they usually do what they do more by native inclination (as in other arts) than by instruction.

The techniques can to some extent be acquired but sincerity is very important. You can pretend to feel that concern for others which evokes a confident response from them but it is the genuine people who manage best. If you are a mountebank you have to be a very good mountebank indeed. Even a high degree of professional skill may be insufficient to safeguard your position as a leader if you affect a degree of concern you do not feel and are caught out.

People who are good at all this often seem to possess innate qualities, elusive, difficult to define but clearly recognizable, rather like that personal attractiveness sometimes described as charm. There may be common characteristics here. I recall the report written on the gay young Earl, now recently retired from his service: 'This young officer is a notable leader of men,' it said. 'Unfortunately he is almost equally successful as a follower of women.'

The value of coercion on the battlefield has always seemed to me rather doubtful. Could Alexander really have taken an army from Attica to the Indus under the whip alone? I doubt it. Was the brutal rigour of Frederick the Great's discipline the only or even the chief secret of his success at Rossbach and Leuthen? Or were the bloody backs of British Redcoats in the eighteenth century the real cause of their performance, say, at Minden? I doubt this.

Military leadership has always been in high degree manipulative. What has changed in our generation is the material, but only in accident, not in essence. The points at which you can handle it differ. The method of manipulation has tended to change.

Thinking of manipulation, of what makes men tick, brings me to another recollection of the desert which may also be relevant. A young officer was wandering about on his feet near me in a not very closely contested tank engagement. I do not think he had been brewed up. As far as I can remember he was in charge of some transport and had lost it. He climbed up on my tank for company, it seemed, more than anything and I could see that he was badly shaken. He was in fact terrified and needed to be given something to do. But I also guessed that if he knew that I knew he was frightened, he would break down, and it would be impossible to keep this knowledge from him if we looked each other in the eye. I gave him a matter-of-fact task somewhere safe, without looking at him, and off he went. When we met that evening I could safely look at him again. He had recovered for the time being and was able to go on and be useful for several more days.

I learned something here, and thereafter used to advise the inexperienced young officer: 'Never look a frightened man in the eye if you want to keep him going.' Of course, it occurs to me now that this can operate the other way round too. One can also be found out oneself in this way.

If I wanted to generalize here I should say that when the failure is failure to control fear, disclosure by a superior of an awareness of a subordinate's failure is usually quite fatal to his further effectiveness. It can even be fatal to disclose that you acknowledge the possibility of such a failure. I am speaking of fear, but I should be surprised if something of the sort were not also true of other possible causes of failure.

Where skills evolve, in my own profession at any rate, some renewal of contact with the lower levels of practice is highly desirable. Such renewals not only help the manager to make better use of technical resources. They do something else. They make a contribution to the coherence of the whole. They help, in industrial terms, to strengthen the communication structure between upper-middle management and the floor of the shop.

Now the coherence of the military group is of the highest possible importance. It is strengthened in armies in every possible way. The whole business of common signs and badges, uniforms, whether you wear your hat straight on or sideways, the whole art of military millinery and all the rest of it is directed to the development of coherence in the group.

It is used first of all to demonstrate a unity of context to the members of the group. It also indicates a difference between this group and other groups

– that this regiment, which wears its hat back to front, is not the same as that, which does not. Once you have established an awareness of difference, of otherness, you are some way towards creating a feeling of betterness, and if you can develop that in your group, your unit, you can jack up your standards. 'This may be good enough,' you can say, 'for those Queens Park Rangers or the Loamshire Fusiliers but it simply will not do in the Fortieth Foot and Mouth,' or the Royal Death Watch, or whatever it happens to be.

The higher the degree of agreement, the wider the area of agreement and the higher the level of common understanding existing between leaders and led (and between the members of each of these two groups too) the greater will be the coherence of the whole organization; the more resistant will it be to stress, the more responsive to direction.

This is the strength of a territorial system in the raising of regiments. Everyone knows and loves the same locality, the same environment. Home is much the same to them all.

There is a great source of strength in the regimental system itself. This sets up in the group a continuing focus of affection, trust and loyalty. It uses insignia, totems and a good deal of almost mystical paraphernalia to increase the binding grip of the whole upon its members. Some day I want to turn the ethnologists on to a study of the regimental system as a means of strengthening group resistance to stress. Their advice may well be that instead of a quaint and decorative traditional survival, we have in the British regimental system a military instrument of deadly efficiency.

Selection procedures both for membership and for promotion and the criteria used in them are of very great importance. The criteria must be relevant to the primary purpose of the enterprise. If selection is against irrelevant criteria the person selected is unlikely to be adequate to the task. It is just worth mentioning here, however, that it is rarely wise to criticize selection procedures and criteria too heavily without prior reflection on the degree of success which the enterprise in question achieves in the discharge of its primary function. It has been suggested, for example, that selection procedures in the Brigade of Guards are on the old-fashioned side and that the criteria need review. This may or may not be true. It is worth remembering, however, that the Brigade of Guards produces fighting infantry without superiors anywhere. This, of course, is its primary function. There are enterprises whose selection procedures can be said to be far more up to date but whose success in their primary function is significantly less.

In this respect the importance of the coherence of the group must again be remembered. The acceptability of one member of the group to the others must not be disregarded.

The high morale of parachute troops is always interesting. It springs from an awareness in every man who has done his jumps of a victory in himself over fear. But there is much more than that. Each man also knows that everyone else has surmounted the same threshold. More important still, he knows that they know this of him too.

One important thing in the leader/follower relationship, it has always seemed to me, is that you get what you give, and no more. You are only really entitled to ask from below what you are prepared to give to those above. Beginners in this game have sometimes thought to acquire prestige with their subordinates by affecting a fine disregard of their superiors. But buying compliance by disloyalty is a short-term expedient which is in the highest degree dangerous.

In the American Civil War, when Abraham Lincoln appointed Hooker to command the army of the Potomac, he was making the best choice he could but he knew Hooker had faults. He knew, for instance, that Hooker had tried to obstruct his predecessor Burnside. In his letter of appointment Lincoln wrote: 'I much fear that the spirit which you have decided to infuse into the army of criticizing their commander and withholding confidence from him will now turn upon you.' This is something worth reflecting on at all levels of responsibility.

I have already expressed doubt on the value in battle of the power of coercion possessed by an officer. It is useful but its usefulness, in relation to battle in modern conditions, rests entirely, in my opinion, on its prior contribution to the creation of a habit – 'Do what the officer says'. Habit is useful when under stress and mimesis is a great tool in the formation of habit. The repetition of drill movements, sometimes mocked a little by the ill informed, is a considerable habit-former. In the last resort, perhaps, Orpheus may be a more powerful leader than the drill sergeant, but hosts of men have been carried further under stress than they would otherwise have been able to go by habits formed under the drill sergeant and in no other way.

I think if I were asked to name the most important source of high morale, however, I should say 'adequacy'. If you and your associates are doing something you find worthwhile and know yourselves to be equal to it, and the other requirements are met, like equity and consistency in the way you are handled, your morale will be high. In the Arnhem battle even when we knew we were beat we knew we were better and the structure of the First Airborne Division was never eroded by despair.

But before I go too far away from consideration of what causes one man to follow the immediate lead of another in battle let me call to mind the confidential report once said to have been written on a subaltern by his commanding officer.

'I do not doubt,' it said, 'that there are men who will follow this officer anywhere but, if there are, it will only be out of curiosity.'

In the British Army the man in charge must put first the interests of those over whom he is placed. 'Looking after the men' is a primary principle. When we had animals they were looked after first. The men came after the animals and the officer attended to his own affairs last of all.

I remember how in the last war, in Sicily, a comfortable Foreign Office visitor in a black hat was brought, in some uncertainty, to the H.Q. of the austere Montgomery. Here he found not an anchorite's hut as he had half expected but a palace by the sea, where he was given champagne cocktails for the whole hour or so until he could get into the presence. He expressed his surprise, when they finally met, to the Army Commander. Monty replied, 'It's my Brigadiers. I don't touch the stuff myself. But if I don't give my Brigadiers champagne they won't work.'

An elementary consideration is that a commanding officer, say of an armoured regiment, will make great efforts to ensure that his regiment has all it needs for the job. There are dangers to the whole enterprise, however, from excessive application of what is basically an admirable inclination. In the desert the complicated ancillary equipment which goes with tanks got at one time very short. As a result, when tanks were sent in for repair, the regiments took everything from them they could to make sure that they did not later on go short of items which they knew were already scarce. When the tank was repaired and issued to someone else there was insufficient of the kit available at the base to fit it out completely. It arrived in the next unit with deficiencies. This reinforced the general inclination to see that no tank went back for repair with anything on it that could be taken off. Thus the cycle proceeded, to the grave detriment of the efficiency of the whole enterprise, and only ruthless action at higher level was able to cut into it and restore balance.

Over-insurance, in provision of material support, is a common British military characteristic. We like to take around everything we think we may need and add some more for luck, just as we are inclined to parade for a parade. But where resources (and time) are not unlimited this tendency can only lead to inefficiency and the commander has to watch it very carefully.

A land commander in modern war has to go to a good deal of trouble to make contact with the men under his command. They are widely spread. He has to travel immense distances and suffer many other physical inconveniences to cultivate their acquaintance. In a ship at sea circumstances are in some respects the diametrical opposite. The men under a captain's command are concentrated with him in a small space. Considerable attention is given here to ordering things in such a way that they are kept apart. In this comparison two of the essential elements in military leadership are illustrated. There is the requirement on the one hand to clothe high command with a physical presence known as far as possible at first hand. There is the need on the other to preserve some degree of detachment.

The man with high military responsibilities is often rather shy and may not always welcome the rough, down-to-earth contacts which making himself known to troops (and getting known of them) involves.

He is also often unlucky.

Few commanders have got themselves over to troops under their command more swiftly than Allenby in Palestine. But even he could not escape. He found a soldier picking the lice out of his clothing. 'Ah, picking them out I see,' he said. 'Well not exactly,' said the man, without looking up, 'Really just taking them as they come.'

Montgomery's problem in the early days in the British Eighth Army has always seemed to me a most interesting one, from the time I first saw him tackling it when I was a junior member of the same firm. It is probably a fair thing to say that a new outlook was wanted in the Eighth Army in late summer 1942. We needed to be shaken out of the habit of treating the thing as an endless exercise in extensive warfare with unlimited opportunity for manoeuvre. Now that we were back in the back gardens of Alexandria (and some of us could get in and ride polo ponies we had not seen for months) we had really come to an end of all that.

Some of the fine old military maxims of Eleventh Hussar armoured car commanders operating west of the Nile in the void of the desert were out of date. 'When in doubt, East with a touch of South,' for instance, now no longer applied. We had to stand and fight on the defensive yet again at Alam el Halfa, and no withdrawal from the main position could now be allowed.

All this was to happen under the new regime of Monty, now commanding at a level at which he was very, very good.

Monty set about making himself known, from the Qattara depression to the sea, in a way that shocked some but invigorated more. Here was a man making his own legend to a set design. Here was also someone deliberately stimulating a sense of coherence and identity of purpose.

He first of all made it quite clear that there would be no further withdrawals. He made this clear not only by his orders but in a series of blunt but good-humoured encounters with the troops, which he knew would be widely reported. He got around everywhere and chose the manner of his appearance to suit the occasion. To the Forty-Fourth Home Counties Division, just arrived in the desert, with white knees and (though perhaps my memory embroiders here) solar topees, he went in shorts, beret, suede boots and bush shirt, swinging a flywhisk and telling them they needed desert experience. To us in the Seventh Armoured, the Desert Rats, he came, I recall, in field boots, breeches, service dress tunic, Sam Browne belt, spurs and red hat – a typical British General Officer – and something we had not seen for a very long time. He told us we had been in the desert too long and were getting into a groove.

He was not a convivial man but he was a ready man, with a sharp eye and a sharp tongue, and he certainly made himself known.

But if you weave yourself thoroughly into the fabric of an army, lead it in success and give it an anthropomorphic godhead in your own eccentric image, you must be prepared for the consequences. It will rely upon your presence. About the time the Eighth Army was stoking up for Agheila, with memories of two renewals of the Benghazi handicap, Monty went back to Cairo. Stories going around that he was coming down from some desert peak, after communion in a cloud, bearing new tablets of stone, proved to be unfounded. He contented himself with reading the lesson in the Cathedral. But I seem to remember Freddy de Guingand, who was then his Chief of Staff, telling me that there was a little anxiety whether the confidence of the troops at this critical point in the desert campaign might not suffer if master stayed too long away. A telegram was accordingly sent which brought him up to the desert again some days before he had intended to come.

I remember, too, an occasion in Italy several months later. Monty was talking to a spellbound group, which included myself as a young commander of a brigade then resting, who had drifted up to see his old desert friends. The Eighth Army Commander was explaining what would be the command set-up for 'Overlord', the assault on north-west Europe.

Marshall would be Supreme Commander (he was not right there of course), he himself would command the assault (no one had actually invited him, but here he was right), and so on.

'What about Eighth Army?' said someone, 'who will command Eighth Army then?'

'Eighth Army?' said Monty. 'Anyone can have Eighth Army.'

Does this sound brutal? Perhaps it does, but it also illustrates a main characteristic of military leadership. I think of it as the principle of total engagement. A man only really gets the best out of the men he commands by something approaching a complete fusion of his own identity with the corporate whole they form. He *is* the Eighth Army, or No. 2 troop of C Squadron, or whatever it is. He is its living personification for so long as he remains its leader. When the time comes for him to leave it he extracts himself completely – to engage himself totally in whatever he is put to next. People can be hurt here. They can be left hurt and lost, while the leader goes on untouched. To lessen the effect of what is an unavoidable operation, and can be a painful one, a high degree of imagination is often needed. It is not always found. This happens, in the army, in peace as well as in war. In war the extractions are more sudden, more savage, and the emotional pressures are greater. But the engagement of the individual's loyalty to the task in hand, and to the people committed to his care and direction for its discharge, is no less total in peace than in war.

Is the principle of total engagement not fundamental in all of man's more serious activities, whether in peace or war, in whatever part of the world, in man's whole history? I believe it is.

Notes

I   *Origins of a Profession*

1 Andrzejewski (*Military Organization and Society*, 1954, p. 127) uses this term to describe a society in which the distribution of what are believed to be benefits is determined only by naked force.
2 H. D. Lasswell, *The Analysis of Political Behaviour*, 1947, p. 152.
3 Plutarch, *Lycurgus*, passim.
4 Herodotus, IX, 28, 8.
5 op. cit., 15.
6 A. W. Gomme, *A Historical Commentary on Thucydides*, 1945, vol. I, p. 14 f.
7 cit. A. Vagts, *A History of Militarism*, 1938, p. 35.
8 This at any rate is Herodotus' account of the arrangement. Modern scholars tend to doubt his version.
9 H. M. D. Parker, *The Roman Legions*, 1928, p. 235 ff. I rely generally on Parker for what follows.
10 Vegetius, *Epitoma Rei Militaris*, I, 23. Extensive extracts are quoted in translation by Major T. R. Phillips, *Roots of Strategy*, 1943.
11 ibid., III, 26.
12 Tacitus, *Annals*, XI, 18.
13 ibid., I, 23.
14 Vegetius, op. cit., II, 8.
15 ibid., II, 20.
16 p. 22.
17 C. Dufresnoy, *Des Officiers Parlent*, cit. *Survival* (Institute for Strategic Studies), 4, I, 24.
18 Von Domaszewski, *Die Rangordnung des römischen Heeres*, Bonn, 1908, p. 48, cit. Parker, op. cit., p. 206.

19 *Epitoma Rei Militaris*, or *De Re Militari*.

II   *Knights and Mercenaries*

20 Lynn White Jr., *Medieval technology and social change*, 1962, p. 29.
21 A useful examination of the evidence on the introduction of the stirrup into Western Europe can be found in Lynn White, op. cit., chap. I. Perhaps the first mention of it in literature is in the *Strategikon* of the emperor Maurice (582–602).
22 J. U. Nef, *War and Human Progress*, 1950, p. 32.
23 F. Lot, *L'Art Militaire et les Armées au Moyen Age*, 1946, vol. II, p. 442.
24 D. M. Bueno de Mesquita, 'Some Condottieri of the Trecento', *Proceedings of the British Academy*, vol. XXXII, 1946, p. 219.
25 cit. E. M. Earle, *Makers of Modern Strategy*, Princeton, 1944, p. 12, to whom I am indebted for much of what follows.
26 M. Roberts, *The Military Revolution 1560–1660* (Inaugural Lecture, Queen's University, Belfast), p. 8.
27 op. cit., pp. 27–8.
28 Nef, op. cit., p. 28.
29 Sir J. Turner, *Pallas Armata*, 1670, p. 174.
30 Roberts, op. cit., p. 21.

III   *Armies of the Nation State*

31 Nef, op. cit., p. 202.

32 Another term of Andrzejewski's.
33 A. Babeau, *La vie militaire sous l'ancien régime*, 1889, vol. I, p. 20. Babeau is my principal authority for this period.

IV   *Prussia and Napoleon*

34 *The History of the Decline and Fall of the Roman Empire*, ed. Smith, 1854, vol. IV, p. 405 ff.
35 'An Essay upon Projects', in H. Morley, *The Earlier Life . . . of Daniel Defoe*, 1889, p. 135.
36 For a lower estimate (14%) cf. Lt.-Col. G. F. R. Henderson, *Stonewall Jackson*, 1902, p. 499.
37 *Les Rêveries . . . de Maurice Comte de Saxe*, The Hague, 1756, p. 215. See also in Phillips, op. cit., p. 161.
38 Nef, op. cit., p. 237.
39 *Cambridge Modern History*, vol. VI, p. 215.
40 One of his commands, quoted in vol. viii of *The New Cambridge Modern History* (p. 181) was as follows: 'If a soldier during an action looks about as if to fly, or so much as sets foot outside the line, the non-commissioned officer standing behind him will run him through with his bayonet and kill him on the spot.'
41 *The Luck of Barry Lyndon, Esq.*, 1892, p. 44 f.
42 'Essai Général de Tactique' (most accessible in vols. I and II of his *Oeuvres Militaires*, 1803), vol. I, p. 13. Earle translates the main

passages, op. cit., pp. 62–6.
43 Nef, op. cit., p. 306.
44 ibid., p. 251.
45 *Die Instruktion Friedrichs des Grossen für seine Generale von 1747*, Berlin, 1936, p. 2. A French translation is opposite the German. See also Phillips, op. cit., p. 167.
46 Thackeray, op. cit., p. 45.
47 vide Nef, op. cit., p. 234.
48 vide note 42 above.
49 H. Lloyd, *History of the Late War in Germany*, 1781, part II, preface, p. 7, cit. S. P. Huntington, *The Soldier and the State*, Cambridge (Mass.), 1957, p. 30.
50 cit. J. W. Wheeler-Bennett, *The Nemesis of Power*, New York, 1953, Introduction, p. vii.
51 *Die Instruktion*, etc., p. 5. See also Phillips op. cit.
52 Vagts, op. cit., p. 112 f., on whom much of what follows is based.
53 Nef, op. cit., p. 318 f.
54 Goethe, *Die Campagne in Frankreich 1792*, Paris, 1868, p. 77. An English translation by R. Farie, London, 1849, p. 81. The passage from 19 to 22 September is of high significance and well worth reading in extenso.

V The Nineteenth-Century Officer

55 Blücher, *Briefe*, Stuttgart, 1913, p. 85, letter of 3 August 1807 to Gneisenau.
56 cit. Huntington, op. cit., p. 31.
57 M. Lehmann, *Scharnhorst*, Leipzig, vol. I, p. 323, and vol. II, pp. 110 and 197, cit. Vagts, op. cit., p. 142.
58 Vagts, op. cit., p. 145.
59 *Deutsche Vierteljahrschrift*, 1859, No. 2, p. 69, cit. Vagts, op. cit., p. 242.
60 Huntington, op. cit., p. 52.
61 L. Wraxall, *The Armies of the Great Powers*, 1859, pp. 99–100, cit. Huntington, op. cit., p. 53.
62 G. M. Young, *Victorian England*, 1953, p. 98 (Dr Kitson Clark showed me this).
63 Huntington, op. cit., p. 47.
64 Viscount Wolseley, *The Standing Army of Great Britain*, Harper's, New York, LXXX (Feb. 1890), pp. 331–347, cit. Huntington, op. cit., p. 53.
65 Sir J. Fortescue, *History of the British Army*, 1899, vol. X, p. 225, cit. Vagts, op. cit., p. 156.
66 Huntington, op. cit., p. 43.
67 cit. R. Lewis and A. Maude, *Professional People*, 1952, p. 31.
68 George Mason, cit. Huntington, op. cit., p. 165.
69 Huntington, op. cit., p. 195 f. I follow Huntington closely for this period.
70 Pascal, *Pensées*, 169–298. In *Oeuvres Complètes*, 1931, p. 102.
71 Power, 1938, p. 277.
72 op. cit., p. 37.
73 *Revue des Deux Mondes*, 15 March 1891, p. 443 ff. Republished as *Du Rôle Social de l'Officier*, Julliard, 1946.

VI Society and the Soldier: 1914–18

74 W. Wenck, *Deutschland vor Hundert Jahren*, 1887, vol. I, p. 61, quoting a writer of 1785.
75 Aristotle, *Politics*, bk. 1, chap. 2, and bk. 3, chap. 6. An English translation by Jowett, Oxford, 1905.
76 A. Toynbee, *A Study of History*, 1939, vol. IV, p. 640.
77 It is going too far to suggest, as Evelyn Waugh does in *Men at Arms*, that where there are gentlemen in charge of military operations conducted under stress there will be order and where there are not there will be none. To maintain this is to adhere to the eighteenth-century notion that the qualities essential in the good officer will only be found in 'gentlemen', using the term, as Waugh seems to, in its eighteenth-century connotation.
78 cit. Toynbee, op. cit., p. 644.
79 Kant, *Zum Ewigen Frieden*, Königsberg, 1795, p. 57, quoting an unnamed Greek. An English translation by M. Campbell Smith, London, 1903.
80 cf. M. Janowitz, *The Professional Soldier*, Free Press of Glencoe, 1960, pp. 108–121.
81 cit. Janowitz, op. cit., p. 223.
82 G. Mayer, *Friedrich Engels*, The Hague, 1934, vol. II, p. 436, cit. Vagts, op. cit., p. 227. An English translation by G. & H. Highet, London, 1936.
83 B. H. Liddell Hart, *Foch*, 1931, p. 474.
84 ibid., p. 67.
85 J. Monteilhet, *Les Institutions Militaires de la France*, 1932, p. 262.
86 vide Liddell Hart, op. cit., p. 47.
87 Monteilhet, op. cit., p. 321.
88 Major-General J. F. C. Fuller, *The Conduct of War 1789–1961*, 1961, p. 142.
89 B. W. Tuchman, *August 1914*, 1962, p. 425.
90 Nef, op. cit., p. 367.
91 Tuchman, op. cit., p. 241.
92 cit. Alan Clark, *The Donkeys*, 1961, p. 163. The minute is dated 14 April 1915.
93 Toynbee, op. cit., vol. IV, p. 153.
94 S. Sassoon, *Collected Poems*, 1947, p. 75.
95 vide note 59, chapter V above.

VII Today and Tomorrow

96 Sterne, *A Sentimental Journey*, 1768, p. 120 ff.
97 'It was reserved to the genius of Napoleon to make unmannerly war.' Bülow, cit. Vagts, op. cit., p. 91.
98 see note 34, chapter IV above.
99 It would be idle to pretend that a dilemma cannot arise here. The French forces in Syria and Lebanon, the Troupes Françaises du Levant, after the fall of France, fought the British, their former allies, who were prosecuting the war against Germany. They did this on the orders of a metropolitan government: it had capitulated, but their duty as professionals still lay to a government whose legitimacy they could not question. On the other hand many German professional officers who detested Nazism were unable to deny that legitimate authority in Germany lay with the Nazis. They therefore continued to

fight against the Allies, in whose victory lay the only hope for Germany, as many knew. They were, of course, much helped in their confusion by the insistence of the Allies that the German nation was their enemy, and not only the German government.

100 *Putnam's Monthly*, New York, vol. VI, 1855, pp. 193–206 and 306–31. Cit. Rapoport, 'A comparative theory of military and political types', in *Changing Patterns of Military Politics*, ed. S. P. Huntington, Free Press of Glencoe, 1962, p. 71.

101 The U.S. Army in the twentieth century: the volume of published material on organization, management, leadership, professionalism, career structure and related areas of interest in U.S. Army practice is enormous. In assembling source material for what is contained in this chapter I have relied greatly on the advice of Lt Col. Charles Shrader of the U.S. Army Military History Institute and his colleague Lt Col. D. F. Frasché whose assistance and friendship have been of high value to me. I have found the following of particular interest: *From Root to Macnamara* by James E. Hewes; *Americans at War* by T. Harry Williams (especially chapter 3); *Arms and Men* by Walter Willis; *An Army for Empire* by Graham A. Cosmos (early chapters); and *Military Professionalism and Officership in America* by Allan R. Millett, which includes a good bibliography and notes on the impact of technology and business in the U.S. Army.

I read with close and sympathetic attention much that has been written by General E. C. Meyer, Chief of Staff of the Army, whose efforts to correct aberration in U.S. Army practice command admiration and respect. Typical of much of General Meyer's writing is an article on 'Unit Cohesion . . . the Ingredient for Success' written for the magazine published by the Department of Defense, *Defense 81*.

I have also made grateful use of lecture notes and other material furnished by Lt Col. Shrader (who is not only a good soldier but a respectable mediaevalist) and Lt Col. Frasché.

102 *The Armed Forces Officer*, Department of Defense, Washington, 1950, p. 4, cit. Janowitz, op. cit., p. 219.

103 Janowitz (op. cit., p. 79) is interesting on this point.

104 *The People*, 1 July 1962, p. 10.

105 Defence White Paper, 1960.

106 I should be inclined to describe them as abanausic.

107 vide *Candide*, passim.

108 Francis Quarles, Epigram.

109 Cicero, *De Officiis*, bk. I, chap. 5, secc. 15–17.

110 *Authority and the Individual* (Reith Lectures, 1948–9), 1949, p. 111.

Index

Illustration Acknowledgements

The author and publishers are grateful to the following for providing and/or granting permission to reproduce the illustrations on the pages listed:

2, Photographie Bulloz, Paris; 6, The Pierpont Morgan Library, New York; 8, The Mansell Collection; 11, Wadsworth Atheneum; 12, The Mansell Collection; 13, Peter Newark's Historical Pictures; 14, The Mansell Collection; 15, The Mansell Collection; 16–17, The Mansell Collection; 18, Deutscher Archaelogischen Institut; 19, Anderson; 20, Deutscher Archaelogischen Institut; 23, The Mansell Collection; 24, Ciccione-Bulloz; 26, Photographie Bulloz, Paris; 27, The Mansell Collection; 28, Department of the Environment (Crown Copyright); 29 top, Photographie Bulloz, Paris; 29 bottom, Peter Newark's Historical Pictures; 30, The Mansell Collection; 31, The Mansell Collection; 32, Peter Newark's Historical Pictures; 33 top, Editorial Photocolor Archives Inc.; 33 bottom, Michael Holford/British Museum; 34 top and bottom, Michael Holford/British Museum; 35 top and bottom, Michael Holford/British Museum; 36, Biblioteca del Monasterio de el Escorial, Madrid; 37 top, Photographie Bulloz, Paris; 37 bottom, Musée de l'Arsenal, Paris; 38 top and bottom, Photographie Giraudon, Paris; 39, Photographie Giraudon, Paris; 40 top and bottom, Bridgeman Art Library; 44, The Mansell Collection; 46, The Mansell Collection; 47 top pictures, Peter Newark's Historical Pictures; 47 bottom, The Mansell Collection; 49, Studios Josse Lalance & Cie; 50, The Pierpont Morgan Library, New York; 51, Peter Newark's Historical Pictures; 53, The Folgar Shakespeare Library, Washington D.C.; 54–5, The Mansell Collection; 56, The Mansell Collection; 57, The Mansell Collection; 58, The Mansell Collection; 60, Ullstein Bilderdienst; 62–3, Photographie Bulloz, Paris; 64, Ullstein Bilderdienst; 65, Photographie Bulloz, Paris; 66, Photographie Bulloz, Paris; 67, Photographie Bulloz, Paris; 68, Peter Newark's Historical Pictures; 69, Ullstein Bilderdienst; 70–1, Bildarchiv Preussischer Kulturbesitz; 72, Editorial Photocolor Archives, Inc.; 74, Mansell-Bulloz; 76–7, The Mansell Collection; 78, The Mansell Collection; 79, Peter Newark's Historical Pictures; 80, Ullstein Bilderdienst; 80–1, Photographie Bulloz, Paris; 81, Peter Newark's Historical Pictures; 82, Bildarchiv Preussischer Kulturbesitz; 83, Bildarchiv Preussischer Kulturbesitz; 84, Peter Newark's Historical Pictures; 85, Ullstein Bilderdienst; 91, Peter Newark's Historical Pictures; 92–3, The Mansell Collection; 94, Anne Horton; 95, Roger-Viollet; 96, Peter Newark's Historical Pictures; 97, The Mansell Collection; 98, Bildarchiv Preussischer Kulturbesitz; 100, Ullstein Bilderdienst; 102, Ullstein Bilderdienst; 103, Novosti Press Agency; 105 top, Photographie Giraudon, Paris; 105 bottom, Peter Newark's Historical Pictures; 106 (all pictures), Peter Newark's Historical Pictures; 107 top, The Bridgeman Art Library; 107 bottom, Photographie Giraudon, Paris; 108, Photographie Giraudon, Paris; 109 top, The Bridgeman Art Library; 109 bottom, Peter Newark's Historical Pictures; 110 top and bottom, Sidgwick and Jackson; 111 top, Peter Newark's Historical Pictures; 111 bottom, The Mansell Collection; 112, Peter Newark's Historical Pictures; 113, Peter Newark's Historical Pictures; 114 top and bottom, Photographie Giraudon, Paris; 115 top, Photographie Giraudon, Paris; 115 bottom, Anne Horton; 116 top, Peter Newark's Historical Pictures; 116 bottom, Historisches Museum, Rastatt/Life Magazine; 117 top, The Bridgeman Art Library; 117 bottom, Peter Newark's Western Americana; 118 top and bottom, Peter Newark's Historical Pictures; 119 top and bottom, Peter Newark's Historical Pictures; 120 top and bottom, The Bridgeman Art Library; 122, The Mansell Collection; 123, The Mansell Collection; 128, Library of Congress, Washington D.C.; 129, Library of Congress, Washington D.C.; 130, Anne Horton; 131, Popperfoto; 132, Popperfoto; 136–7, The Mansell Collection; 138, Robert Hunt Library; 140, The Mansell Collection; 142, The Mansell Collection; 143, Peter Newark's Historical Pictures; 144–5, United Press International; 147, Peter Newark's Historical Pictures; 148, National Archives, Washington D.C.; 149, Popperfoto; 150–1, Imperial War Museum; 152, French Government Tourist Office; 153, Library of Congress, Washington D.C.; 154 top, Roger-Viollet; 154 bottom, United Press International; 155, International News Photos; 156, Imperial War Museum; 158–9, Popperfoto; 160, U.P.I. Radiophoto by John Schneider; 162, Popperfoto; 163, Popperfoto; 164, Robert Hunt Library; 165, Imperial War Museum; 166, Uitgeverej D.E., N.V. de Arbeiderspers, Amsterdam; 169, Popperfoto; 170, Robert Hunt Library; 171, Popperfoto; 172, United States Army; 173, Robert Hunt Library; 175 top and bottom, Public Relations Photo Section, Northern Army Group; 176, Popperfoto; 177, United Press International (photo by Nick Wheeler); 178–9, United Press International; 180, Peter Newark's Western Americana; 181, Peter Newark's Western Americana; 182–3, Library of Congress, Washington D.C.; 185, Peter Newark's Western Americana; 186–7, Peter Newark's Western Americana; 188, Robert Hunt Library; 189 top, Peter Newark's Historical Pictures; 189 bottom, John Launois, Black Star; 190, Peter Newark's Western Americana; 191, Peter Newark's Western Americana; 192, Peter Newark's Western Americana; 193 left and right, Popperfoto; 194, Peter Newark's Western Americana; 196, Robert Hunt Library; 198, Time Inc. (photo by Terry Smith); 200, Robert Hunt Library; 201, Public Relations Photo Section, Northern Army Group; 203 top, Sir John Hackett's private collection; 203 bottom, Sir John Hackett's private collection (photo by T.W. Francklin); 204, Sir John Hackett's private collection; 209, Popperfoto; 210, Robert Hunt Library; 212–13, Popperfoto.